AI
Self-Driving Cars
Momentum

Practical Advances in
Artificial Intelligence and Machine Learning

Dr. Lance B. Eliot, MBA, PhD

ISBN: 1-7332498-6-7
ISBN-13: 978-1-7332498-6-7

DEDICATION

To my incredible daughter, Lauren, and my incredible son, Michael.

Forest fortuna adiuvat (from the Latin; good fortune favors the brave).

CONTENTS

Lance B. Eliot

ACKNOWLEDGMENTS

I have been the beneficiary of advice and counsel by many friends, colleagues, family, investors, and many others. I want to thank everyone that has aided me throughout my career. I write from the heart and the head, having experienced first-hand what it means to have others around you that support you during the good times and the tough times.

To Warren Bennis, one of my doctoral advisors and ultimately a colleague, I offer my deepest thanks and appreciation, especially for his calm and insightful wisdom and support.

To Mark Stevens and his generous efforts toward funding and supporting the USC Stevens Center for Innovation.

To Lloyd Greif and the USC Lloyd Greif Center for Entrepreneurial Studies for their ongoing encouragement of founders and entrepreneurs.

To Peter Drucker, William Wang, Aaron Levie, Peter Kim, Jon Kraft, Cindy Crawford, Jenny Ming, Steve Milligan, Chis Underwood, Frank Gehry, Buzz Aldrin, Steve Forbes, Bill Thompson, Dave Dillon, Alan Fuerstman, Larry Ellison, Jim Sinegal, John Sperling, Mark Stevenson, Anand Nallathambi, Thomas Barrack, Jr., and many other innovators and leaders that I have met and gained mightily from doing so.

Thanks to Ed Trainor, Kevin Anderson, James Hickey, Wendell Jones, Ken Harris, DuWayne Peterson, Mike Brown, Jim Thornton, Abhi Beniwal, Al Biland, John Nomura, Eliot Weinman, John Desmond, and many others for their unwavering support during my career.

And most of all thanks as always to Lauren and Michael, for their ongoing support and for having seen me writing and heard much of this material during the many months involved in writing it. To their patience and willingness to listen.

INTRODUCTION

This is a book that provides the newest innovations and the latest Artificial Intelligence (AI) advances about the emerging nature of AI-based autonomous self-driving driverless cars. Via recent advances in Artificial Intelligence (AI) and Machine Learning (ML), we are nearing the day when vehicles can control themselves and will not require and nor rely upon human intervention to perform their driving tasks (or, that <u>allow</u> for human intervention, but only *require* human intervention in very limited ways).

Similar to my other related books, which I describe in a moment and list the chapters in the Appendix A of this book, I am particularly focused on those advances that pertain to self-driving cars. The phrase "autonomous vehicles" is often used to refer to any kind of vehicle, whether it is ground-based or in the air or sea, and whether it is a cargo hauling trailer truck or a conventional passenger car. Though the aspects described in this book are certainly applicable to all kinds of autonomous vehicles, I am focused more so here on cars.

Indeed, I am especially known for my role in aiding the advancement of self-driving cars, serving currently as the Executive Director of the Cybernetic AI Self-Driving Cars Institute. In addition to writing software, designing and developing systems and software for self-driving cars, I also speak and write quite a bit about the topic. This book is a collection of some of my more advanced essays. For those of you that might have seen my essays posted elsewhere, I have updated them and integrated them into this book as one handy cohesive package.

You might be interested in companion books that I have written that provide additional key innovations and fundamentals about self-driving cars. Those books are entitled **"Introduction to Driverless Self-Driving Cars," "Advances in AI and Autonomous Vehicles: Cybernetic Self-Driving Cars," "Self-Driving Cars: "The Mother of All AI Projects," "Innovation and Thought Leadership on Self-Driving Driverless Cars," "New Advances in AI Autonomous Driverless Self-Driving Cars," "Autonomous Vehicle Driverless Self-Driving Cars and Artificial Intelligence," "Transformative Artificial Intelligence**

Driverless Self-Driving Cars," "Disruptive Artificial Intelligence and Driverless Self-Driving Cars, and "State-of-the-Art AI Driverless Self-Driving Cars," and "Top Trends in AI Self-Driving Cars," and "AI Innovations and Self-Driving Cars," "Crucial Advances for AI Driverless Cars," "Sociotechnical Insights and AI Driverless Cars," "Pioneering Advances for AI Driverless Cars" and "Leading Edge Trends for AI Driverless Cars," "The Cutting Edge of AI Autonomous Cars" and "The Next Wave of AI Self-Driving Cars" and "Revolutionary Innovations of AI Self-Driving Cars," and "AI Self-Driving Cars Breakthroughs," "Trailblazing Trends for AI Self-Driving Cars," "Ingenious Strides for AI Driverless Cars," "AI Self-Driving Cars Inventiveness," "Visionary Secrets of AI Driverless Cars," "Spearheading AI Self-Driving Cars," "Spurring AI Self-Driving Cars," "Avant-Garde AI Driverless Cars," "AI Self-Driving Cars Evolvement," "AI Driverless Cars Chrysalis," "Boosting AI Autonomous Cars," "AI Self-Driving Cars Trendsetting," "AI Autonomous Cars Forefront, "AI Autonomous Cars Emergence," "AI Autonomous Cars Progress," "AI Self-Driving Cars Prognosis," "AI Self-Driving Cars Momentum" (they are available on Amazon). Appendix A has a listing of the chapters covered.

For this book, I am going to borrow my introduction from those companion books, since it does a good job of laying out the landscape of self-driving cars and my overall viewpoints on the topic. The remainder of this book is material that does not appear in the companion books.

INTRODUCTION TO SELF-DRIVING CARS

This is a book about self-driving cars. Someday in the future, we'll all have self-driving cars and this book will perhaps seem antiquated, but right now, we are at the forefront of the self-driving car wave. Daily news bombards us with flashes of new announcements by one car maker or another and leaves the impression that within the next few weeks or maybe months that the self-driving car will be here. A casual non-technical reader would assume from these news flashes that in fact we must be on the cusp of a true self-driving car. Here's a real news flash: We are still quite a distance from having a true self-driving car. It is years to go before we get there.

A true self-driving car is akin to a moonshot. In the same manner that getting us to the moon was an incredible feat, likewise is achieving a true self-driving car. Anybody that suggests or even brashly states that the true self-driving car is nearly here should be viewed with great skepticism. Indeed, you'll see that I often tend to use the word "hogwash" or "crock" when I assess much of the decidedly *fake news* about self-driving cars.

Indeed, I've been writing a popular blog post about self-driving cars and hitting hard on those that try to wave their hands and pretend that we are on the imminent verge of true self-driving cars. For many years, I've been known as the AI Insider. Besides writing about AI, I also develop AI software. I do what I describe. It also gives me insights into what others that are doing AI are really doing versus what it is said they are doing.

Many faithful readers had asked me to pull together my insightful short essays and put them into another book, which you are now holding.

For those of you that have been reading my essays over the years, this collection not only puts them together into one handy package, I also updated the essays and added new material. For those of you that are new to the topic of self-driving cars and AI, I hope you find these essays approachable and informative. I also tend to have a writing style with a bit of a voice, and so you'll see that I am times have a wry sense of humor and poke at conformity.

As a former professor and founder of an AI research lab, I for many years wrote in the formal language of academic writing. I published in referred journals and served as an editor for several AI journals. This writing here is not of the nature, and I have adopted a different and more informal style for these essays. That being said, I also do mention from time-to-time more rigorous material on AI and encourage you all to dig into those deeper and more formal materials if so interested.

I am also an AI practitioner. This means that I write AI software for a living. Currently, I head-up the Cybernetics Self-Driving Car Institute, where we are developing AI software for self-driving cars. I am excited to also report that my son, also a software engineer, heads-up our Cybernetics Self-Driving Car Lab. What I have helped to start, and for which he is an integral part, ultimately he will carry long into the future after I have retired. My daughter, a marketing whiz, also is integral to our efforts as head of our Marketing group. She too will carry forward the legacy now being formulated.

For those of you that are reading this book and have a penchant for writing code, you might consider taking a look at the open source code available for self-driving cars. This is a handy place to start learning how to develop AI for self-driving cars. There are also many new educational courses spring forth. There is a growing body of those wanting to learn about and develop self-driving cars, and a growing body of colleges, labs, and other avenues by which you can learn about self-driving cars.

This book will provide a foundation of aspects that I think will get you ready for those kinds of more advanced training opportunities. If you've already taken those classes, you'll likely find these essays especially interesting as they offer a perspective that I am betting few other instructors or faculty offered to you. These are challenging essays that ask you to think beyond the conventional about self-driving cars.

THE MOTHER OF ALL AI PROJECTS

In June 2017, Apple CEO Tim Cook came out and finally admitted that Apple has been working on a self-driving car. As you'll see in my essays, Apple was enmeshed in secrecy about their self-driving car efforts. We have only been able to read the tea leaves and guess at what Apple has been up to. The notion of an iCar has been floating for quite a while, and self-driving engineers and researchers have been signing tight-lipped Non-Disclosure Agreements (NDA's) to work on projects at Apple that were as shrouded in mystery as any military invasion plans might be.

Tim Cook said something that many others in the Artificial Intelligence (AI) field have been saying, namely, the creation of a self-driving car has got to be the mother of all AI projects. In other words, it is in fact a tremendous moonshot for AI. If a self-driving car can be crafted and the AI works as we hope, it means that we have made incredible strides with AI and that therefore it opens many other worlds of potential breakthrough accomplishments that AI can solve.

Is this hyperbole? Am I just trying to make AI seem like a miracle worker and so provide self-aggrandizing statements for those of us writing the AI software for self-driving cars? No, it is not hyperbole. Developing a true self-driving car is really, really, really hard to do. Let me take a moment to explain why. As a side note, I realize that the Apple CEO is known for at times uttering hyperbole, and he had previously said for example that the year 2012 was "the mother of all years," and he had said that the release of iOS 10 was "the mother of all releases" – all of which does suggest he likes to use the handy "mother of" expression. But, I assure you, in terms of true self-driving cars, he has hit the nail on the head. For sure.

When you think about a moonshot and how we got to the moon, there are some identifiable characteristics and those same aspects can be applied to creating a true self-driving car. You'll notice that I keep putting the word "true" in front of the self-driving car expression. I do so because as per my essay about the various levels of self-driving cars, there are some self-driving cars that are only somewhat of a self-driving car. The somewhat versions are ones that require a human driver to be ready to intervene. In my view, that's not a true self-driving car. A true self-driving car is one that requires no human driver intervention at all. It is a car that can entirely undertake via automation the driving task without any human driver needed. This is the essence of what is known as a Level 5 self-driving car. We are currently at the Level 2 and Level 3 mark, and not yet at Level 5.

4

Getting to the moon involved aspects such as having big stretch goals, incremental progress, experimentation, innovation, and so on. Let's review how this applied to the moonshot of the bygone era, and how it applies to the self-driving car moonshot of today.

Big Stretch Goal

Trying to take a human and deliver the human to the moon, and bring them back, safely, was an extremely large stretch goal at the time. No one knew whether it could be done. The technology wasn't available yet. The cost was huge. The determination would need to be fierce. Etc. To reach a Level 5 self-driving car is going to be the same. It is a big stretch goal. We can readily get to the Level 3, and we are able to see the Level 4 just up ahead, but a Level 5 is still an unknown as to if it is doable. It should eventually be doable and in the same way that we thought we'd eventually get to the moon, but when it will occur is a different story.

Incremental Progress

Getting to the moon did not happen overnight in one fell swoop. It took years and years of incremental progress to get there. Likewise for self-driving cars. Google has famously been striving to get to the Level 5, and pretty much been willing to forgo dealing with the intervening levels, but most of the other self-driving car makers are doing the incremental route. Let's get a good Level 2 and a somewhat Level 3 going. Then, let's improve the Level 3 and get a somewhat Level 4 going. Then, let's improve the Level 4 and finally arrive at a Level 5. This seems to be the prevalent way that we are going to achieve the true self-driving car.

Experimentation

You likely know that there were various experiments involved in perfecting the approach and technology to get to the moon. As per making incremental progress, we first tried to see if we could get a rocket to go into space and safety return, then put a monkey in there, then with a human, then we went all the way to the moon but didn't land, and finally we arrived at the mission that actually landed on the moon. Self-driving cars are the same way. We are doing simulations of self-driving cars. We do testing of self-driving cars on private land under controlled situations. We do testing of self-driving cars on public roadways, often having to meet regulatory requirements including for example having an engineer or equivalent in the car to take over the controls if needed. And so on. Experiments big and small are needed to figure out what works and what doesn't.

Innovation

There are already some advances in AI that are allowing us to progress toward self-driving cars. We are going to need even more advances. Innovation in all aspects of technology are going to be required to achieve a true self-driving car. By no means do we already have everything in-hand that we need to get there. Expect new inventions and new approaches, new algorithms, etc.

Setbacks

Most of the pundits are avoiding talking about potential setbacks in the progress toward self-driving cars. Getting to the moon involved many setbacks, some of which you never have heard of and were buried at the time so as to not dampen enthusiasm and funding for getting to the moon. A recurring theme in many of my included essays is that there are going to be setbacks as we try to arrive at a true self-driving car. Take a deep breath and be ready. I just hope the setbacks don't completely stop progress. I am sure that it will cause progress to alter in a manner that we've not yet seen in the self-driving car field. I liken the self-driving car of today to the excitement everyone had for Uber when it first got going. Today, we have a different view of Uber and with each passing day there are more regulations to the ride sharing business and more concerns raised. The darling child only stays a darling until finally that child acts up. It will happen the same with self-driving cars.

SELF-DRIVING CARS CHALLENGES

But what exactly makes things so hard to have a true self-driving car, you might be asking. You have seen cruise control for years and years. You've lately seen cars that can do parallel parking. You've seen YouTube videos of Tesla drivers that put their hands out the window as their car zooms along the highway, and seen to therefore be in a self-driving car. Aren't we just needing to put a few more sensors onto a car and then we'll have in-hand a true self-driving car? Nope.

Consider for a moment the nature of the driving task. We don't just let anyone at any age drive a car. Worldwide, most countries won't license a driver until the age of 18, though many do allow a learner's permit at the age of 15 or 16. Some suggest that a younger age would be physically too small to reach the controls of the car. Though this might be the case, we could easily adjust the controls to allow for younger aged and thus smaller stature. It's not their physical size that matters. It's their cognitive development that matters.

To drive a car, you need to be able to reason about the car, what the car can and cannot do. You need to know how to operate the car. You need to know about how other cars on the road drive. You need to know what is allowed in driving such as speed limits and driving within marked lanes. You need to be able to react to situations and be able to avoid getting into accidents. You need to ascertain when to hit your brakes, when to steer clear of a pedestrian, and how to keep from ramming that motorcyclist that just cut you off.

Many of us had taken courses on driving. We studied about driving and took driver training. We had to take a test and pass it to be able to drive. The point being that though most adults take the driving task for granted, and we often "mindlessly" drive our cars, there is a significant amount of cognitive effort that goes into driving a car. After a while, it becomes second nature. You don't especially think about how you drive, you just do it. But, if you watch a novice driver, say a teenager learning to drive, you suddenly realize that there is a lot more complexity to it than we seem to realize.

Furthermore, driving is a very serious task. I recall when my daughter and son first learned to drive. They are both very conscientious people. They wanted to make sure that whatever they did, they did well, and that they did not harm anyone. Every day, when you get into a car, it is probably around 4,000 pounds of hefty metal and plastics (about two tons), and it is a lethal weapon. Think about it. You drive down the street in an object that weighs two tons and with the engine it can accelerate and ram into anything you want to hit. The damage a car can inflict is very scary. Both my children were surprised that they were being given the right to maneuver this monster of a beast that could cause tremendous harm entirely by merely letting go of the steering wheel for a moment or taking your eyes off the road.

In fact, in the United States alone there are about 30,000 deaths per year by auto accidents, which is around 100 per day. Given that there are about 263 million cars in the United States, I am actually more amazed that the number of fatalities is not a lot higher. During my morning commute, I look at all the thousands of cars on the freeway around me, and I think that if all of them decided to go zombie and drive in a crazy maniac way, there would be many people dead. Somehow, incredibly, each day, most people drive relatively safely. To me, that's a miracle right there. Getting millions and millions of people to be safe and sane when behind the wheel of a two ton mobile object, it's a feat that we as a society should admire with pride.

So, hopefully you are in agreement that the driving task requires a great deal of cognition. You don't' need to be especially smart to drive a car, and we've done quite a bit to make car driving viable for even the average dolt. There isn't an IQ test that you need to take to drive a car. If you can read and write, and pass a test, you pretty much can legally drive a car. There are of course some that drive a car and are not legally permitted to do so, plus there are private areas such as farms where drivers are young, but for public roadways in the United States, you can be generally of average intelligence (or less) and be able to legally drive.

This though makes it seem like the cognitive effort must not be much. If the cognitive effort was truly hard, wouldn't we only have Einstein's that could drive a car? We have made sure to keep the driving task as simple as we can, by making the controls easy and relatively standardized, and by having roads that are relatively standardized, and so on. It is as though Disneyland has put their Autopia into the real-world, by us all as a society agreeing that roads will be a certain way, and we'll all abide by the various rules of driving.

A modest cognitive task by a human is still something that stymies AI. You certainly know that AI has been able to beat chess players and be good at other kinds of games. This type of narrow cognition is not what car driving is about. Car driving is much wider. It requires knowledge about the world, which a chess playing AI system does not need to know. The cognitive aspects of driving are on the one hand seemingly simple, but at the same time require layer upon layer of knowledge about cars, people, roads, rules, and a myriad of other "common sense" aspects. We don't have any AI systems today that have that same kind of breadth and depth of awareness and knowledge.

As revealed in my essays, the self-driving car of today is using trickery to do particular tasks. It is all very narrow in operation. Plus, it currently assumes that a human driver is ready to intervene. It is like a child that we have taught to stack blocks, but we are needed to be right there in case the child stacks them too high and they begin to fall over. AI of today is brittle, it is narrow, and it does not approach the cognitive abilities of humans. This is why the true self-driving car is somewhere out in the future.

Another aspect to the driving task is that it is not solely a mind exercise. You do need to use your senses to drive. You use your eyes a vision sensors to see the road ahead. You vision capability is like a streaming video, which your brain needs to continually analyze as you drive. Where is the road? Is there a pedestrian in the way? Is there another car ahead of you? Your senses are relying a flood of info to your brain. Self-driving cars are trying to do the same, by using cameras, radar, ultrasound, and lasers. This is an attempt at mimicking how humans have senses and sensory apparatus.

Thus, the driving task is mental and physical. You use your senses, you use your arms and legs to manipulate the controls of the car, and you use your brain to assess the sensory info and direct your limbs to act upon the controls of the car. This all happens instantly. If you've ever perhaps gotten something in your eye and only had one eye available to drive with, you suddenly realize how dependent upon vision you are. If you have a broken foot with a cast, you suddenly realize how hard it is to control the brake pedal and the accelerator. If you've taken medication and your brain is maybe sluggish, you suddenly realize how much mental strain is required to drive a car.

An AI system that plays chess only needs to be focused on playing chess. The physical aspects aren't important because usually a human moves the chess pieces or the chessboard is shown on an electronic display. Using AI for a more life-and-death task such as analyzing MRI images of patients, this again does not require physical capabilities and instead is done by examining images of bits.

Driving a car is a true life-and-death task. It is a use of AI that can easily and at any moment produce death. For those colleagues of mine that are developing this AI, as am I, we need to keep in mind the somber aspects of this. We are producing software that will have in its virtual hands the lives of the occupants of the car, and the lives of those in other nearby cars, and the lives of nearby pedestrians, etc. Chess is not usually a life-or-death matter.

Driving is all around us. Cars are everywhere. Most of today's AI applications involve only a small number of people. Or, they are behind the scenes and we as humans have other recourse if the AI messes up. AI that is driving a car at 80 miles per hour on a highway had better not mess up. The consequences are grave. Multiply this by the number of cars, if we could put magically self-driving into every car in the USA, we'd have AI running in the 263 million cars. That's a lot of AI spread around. This is AI on a massive scale that we are not doing today and that offers both promise and potential peril.

There are some that want AI for self-driving cars because they envision a world without any car accidents. They envision a world in which there is no car congestion and all cars cooperate with each other. These are wonderful utopian visions.

They are also very misleading. The adoption of self-driving cars is going to be incremental and not overnight. We cannot economically just junk all existing cars. Nor are we going to be able to affordably retrofit existing cars. It is more likely that self-driving cars will be built into new cars and that over many years of gradual replacement of existing cars that we'll see the mix of self-driving cars become substantial in the real-world.

In these essays, I have tried to offer technological insights without being overly technical in my description, and also blended the business, societal, and economic aspects too. Technologists need to consider the non-technological impacts of what they do. Non-technologists should be aware of what is being developed.

We all need to work together to collectively be prepared for the enormous disruption and transformative aspects of true self-driving cars. We all need to be involved in this mother of all AI projects.

WHAT THIS BOOK PROVIDES

What does this book provide to you? It introduces many of the key elements about self-driving cars and does so with an AI based perspective. I weave together technical and non-technical aspects, readily going from being concerned about the cognitive capabilities of the driving task and how the technology is embodying this into self-driving cars, and in the next breath I discuss the societal and economic aspects.

They are all intertwined because that's the way reality is. You cannot separate out the technology per se, and instead must consider it within the milieu of what is being invented and innovated, and do so with a mindset towards the contemporary mores and culture that shape what we are doing and what we hope to do.

WHY THIS BOOK

I wrote this book to try and bring to the public view many aspects about self-driving cars that nobody seems to be discussing.

For business leaders that are either involved in making self-driving cars or that are going to leverage self-driving cars, I hope that this book will enlighten you as to the risks involved and ways in which you should be strategizing about how to deal with those risks.

For entrepreneurs, startups and other businesses that want to enter into the self-driving car market that is emerging, I hope this book sparks your interest in doing so, and provides some sense of what might be prudent to pursue.

For researchers that study self-driving cars, I hope this book spurs your interest in the risks and safety issues of self-driving cars, and also nudges you toward conducting research on those aspects.

For students in computer science or related disciplines, I hope this book will provide you with interesting and new ideas and material, for which you might conduct research or provide some career direction insights for you.

For AI companies and high-tech companies pursuing self-driving cars, this book will hopefully broaden your view beyond just the mere coding and development needed to make self-driving cars.

For all readers, I hope that you will find the material in this book to be stimulating. Some of it will be repetitive of things you already know. But I am pretty sure that you'll also find various eureka moments whereby you'll discover a new technique or approach that you had not earlier thought of. I am also betting that there will be material that forces you to rethink some of your current practices.

I am not saying you will suddenly have an epiphany and change what you are doing. I do think though that you will reconsider or perhaps revisit what you are doing.

For anyone choosing to use this book for teaching purposes, please take a look at my suggestions for doing so, as described in the Appendix. I have found the material handy in courses that I have taught, and likewise other faculty have told me that they have found the material handy, in some cases as extended readings and in other instances as a core part of their course (depending on the nature of the class).

In my writing for this book, I have tried carefully to blend both the practitioner and the academic styles of writing. It is not as dense as is typical academic journal writing, but at the same time offers depth by going into the nuances and trade-offs of various practices.

The word "deep" is in vogue today, meaning getting deeply into a subject or topic, and so is the word "unpack" which means to tease out the underlying aspects of a subject or topic. I have sought to offer material that addresses an issue or topic by going relatively deeply into it and make sure that it is well unpacked.

In any book about AI, it is difficult to use our everyday words without having some of them be misinterpreted. Specifically, it is easy to anthropomorphize AI. When I say that an AI system "knows" something, I do not want you to construe that the AI system has sentience and "knows" in the same way that humans do. They aren't that way, as yet. I have tried to use quotes around such words from time-to-time to emphasize that the words I am using should not be misinterpreted to ascribe true human intelligence to the AI systems that we know of today. If I used quotes around all such words, the book would be very difficult to read, and so I am doing so judiciously. Please keep that in mind as you read the material, thanks.

Some of the material is time-based in terms of covering underway activities, and though some of it might decay, nonetheless I believe you'll find the material useful and informative.

COMPANION BOOKS

1. **"Introduction to Driverless Self-Driving Cars"** by Dr. Lance Eliot
2. **"Innovation and Thought Leadership on Self-Driving Driverless Cars"** by Dr. Lance Eliot
3. **"Advances in AI and Autonomous Vehicles: Cybernetic Self-Driving Cars"** by Dr. Lance Eliot
4. **"Self-Driving Cars: The Mother of All AI Projects"** by Dr. Lance Eliot
5. **"New Advances in AI Autonomous Driverless Self-Driving Cars"** by Dr. Lance Eliot
6. **"Autonomous Vehicle Driverless Self-Driving Cars and Artificial Intelligence"** by Dr. Lance Eliot and Michael B. Eliot
7. **"Transformative Artificial Intelligence Driverless Self-Driving Cars"** by Dr. Lance Eliot
8. **"Disruptive Artificial Intelligence and Driverless Self-Driving Cars"** by Dr. Lance Eliot
9. "State-of-the-Art AI Driverless Self-Driving Cars" by Dr. Lance Eliot
10. "Top Trends in AI Self-Driving Cars" by Dr. Lance Eliot
11. **"AI Innovations and Self-Driving Cars"** by Dr. Lance Eliot
12. **"Crucial Advances for AI Driverless Cars"** by Dr. Lance Eliot
13. **"Sociotechnical Insights and AI Driverless Cars"** by Dr. Lance Eliot.
14. **"Pioneering Advances for AI Driverless Cars"** by Dr. Lance Eliot
15. **"Leading Edge Trends for AI Driverless Cars"** by Dr. Lance Eliot
16. **"The Cutting Edge of AI Autonomous Cars"** by Dr. Lance Eliot
17. **"The Next Wave of AI Self-Driving Cars"** by Dr. Lance Eliot
18. **"Revolutionary Innovations of AI Driverless Cars"** by Dr. Lance Eliot
19. **"AI Self-Driving Cars Breakthroughs"** by Dr. Lance Eliot
20. **"Trailblazing Trends for AI Self-Driving Cars"** by Dr. Lance Eliot
21. **"Ingenious Strides for AI Driverless Cars"** by Dr. Lance Eliot
22. **"AI Self-Driving Cars Inventiveness"** by Dr. Lance Eliot
23. **"Visionary Secrets of AI Driverless Cars"** by Dr. Lance Eliot
24. **"Spearheading AI Self-Driving Cars"** by Dr. Lance Eliot
25. **"Spurring AI Self-Driving Cars"** by Dr. Lance Eliot
26. **"Avant-Garde AI Driverless Cars"** by Dr. Lance Eliot
27. **"AI Self-Driving Cars Evolvement"** by Dr. Lance Eliot
28. **"AI Driverless Cars Chrysalis"** by Dr. Lance Eliot
29. **"Boosting AI Autonomous Cars"** by Dr. Lance Eliot
30. **"AI Self-Driving Cars Trendsetting"** by Dr. Lance Eliot
31. **"AI Autonomous Cars Forefront"** by Dr. Lance Eliot
32. **"AI Autonomous Cars Emergence"** by Dr. Lance Eliot
33. **"AI Autonomous Cars Progress"** by Dr. Lance Eliot
34. **"AI Self-Driving Cars Prognosis"** by Dr. Lance Eliot
35. **"AI Self-Driving Cars Momentum"** by Dr. Lance Eliot

These books are available on Amazon and at other major global booksellers.

CHAPTER 1

ELIOT FRAMEWORK FOR AI SELF-DRIVING CARS

CHAPTER 1

ELIOT FRAMEWORK FOR
AI SELF-DRIVING CARS

This chapter is a core foundational aspect for understanding AI self-driving cars and I have used this same chapter in several of my other books to introduce the reader to essential elements of this field. Once you've read this chapter, you'll be prepared to read the rest of the material since the foundational essence of the components of autonomous AI driverless self-driving cars will have been established for you.

When I give presentations about self-driving cars and teach classes on the topic, I have found it helpful to provide a framework around which the various key elements of self-driving cars can be understood and organized (see diagram at the end of this chapter). The framework needs to be simple enough to convey the overarching elements, but at the same time not so simple that it belies the true complexity of self-driving cars. As such, I am going to describe the framework here and try to offer in a thousand words (or more!) what the framework diagram itself intends to portray.

The core elements on the diagram are numbered for ease of reference. The numbering does not suggest any kind of prioritization of the elements. Each element is crucial. Each element has a purpose, and otherwise would not be included in the framework. For some self-driving cars, a particular element might be more important or somehow distinguished in comparison to other self-driving cars.

You could even use the framework to rate a particular self-driving car, doing so by gauging how well it performs in each of the elements of the framework. I will describe each of the elements, one at a time. After doing so, I'll discuss aspects that illustrate how the elements interact and perform during the overall effort of a self-driving car.

At the Cybernetic Self-Driving Car Institute, we use the framework to keep track of what we are working on, and how we are developing software that fills in what is needed to achieve Level 5 self-driving cars.

D-01: Sensor Capture

Let's start with the one element that often gets the most attention in the press about self-driving cars, namely, the sensory devices for a self-driving car.

On the framework, the box labeled as D-01 indicates "Sensor Capture" and refers to the processes of the self-driving car that involve collecting data from the myriad of sensors that are used for a self-driving car. The types of devices typically involved are listed, such as the use of mono cameras, stereo cameras, LIDAR devices, radar systems, ultrasonic devices, GPS, IMU, and so on.

These devices are tasked with obtaining data about the status of the self-driving car and the world around it. Some of the devices are continually providing updates, while others of the devices await an indication by the self-driving car that the device is supposed to collect data. The data might be first transformed in some fashion by the device itself, or it might instead be fed directly into the sensor capture as raw data. At that point, it might be up to the sensor capture processes to do transformations on the data. This all varies depending upon the nature of the devices being used and how the devices were designed and developed.

D-02: Sensor Fusion

Imagine that your eyeballs receive visual images, your nose receives odors, your ears receive sounds, and in essence each of your distinct sensory devices is getting some form of input. The input befits the nature of the device. Likewise, for a self-driving car, the cameras provide visual images, the radar returns radar reflections, and so on.

Each device provides the data as befits what the device does.

At some point, using the analogy to humans, you need to merge together what your eyes see, what your nose smells, what your ears hear, and piece it all together into a larger sense of what the world is all about and what is happening around you. Sensor fusion is the action of taking the singular aspects from each of the devices and putting them together into a larger puzzle.

Sensor fusion is a tough task. There are some devices that might not be working at the time of the sensor capture. Or, there might some devices that are unable to report well what they have detected. Again, using a human analogy, suppose you are in a dark room and so your eyes cannot see much. At that point, you might need to rely more so on your ears and what you hear. The same is true for a self-driving car. If the cameras are obscured due to snow and sleet, it might be that the radar can provide a greater indication of what the external conditions consist of.

In the case of a self-driving car, there can be a plethora of such sensory devices. Each is reporting what it can. Each might have its difficulties. Each might have its limitations, such as how far ahead it can detect an object. All of these limitations need to be considered during the sensor fusion task.

D-03: Virtual World Model

For humans, we presumably keep in our minds a model of the world around us when we are driving a car. In your mind, you know that the car is going at say 60 miles per hour and that you are on a freeway. You have a model in your mind that your car is surrounded by other cars, and that there are lanes to the freeway. Your model is not only based on what you can see, hear, etc., but also what you know about the nature of the world. You know that at any moment that car ahead of you can smash on its brakes, or the car behind you can ram into your car, or that the truck in the next lane might swerve into your lane.

The AI of the self-driving car needs to have a virtual world model, which it then keeps updated with whatever it is receiving from the sensor fusion, which received its input from the sensor capture and the sensory devices.

D-04: System Action Plan

By having a virtual world model, the AI of the self-driving car is able to keep track of where the car is and what is happening around the car. In addition, the AI needs to determine what to do next. Should the self-driving car hit its brakes? Should the self-driving car stay in its lane or swerve into the lane to the left? Should the self-driving car accelerate or slow down?

A system action plan needs to be prepared by the AI of the self-driving car. The action plan specifies what actions should be taken. The actions need to pertain to the status of the virtual world model. Plus, the actions need to be realizable.

This realizability means that the AI cannot just assert that the self-driving car should suddenly sprout wings and fly. Instead, the AI must be bound by whatever the self-driving car can actually do, such as coming to a halt in a distance of X feet at a speed of Y miles per hour, rather than perhaps asserting that the self-driving car come to a halt in 0 feet as though it could instantaneously come to a stop while it is in motion.

D-05: Controls Activation

The system action plan is implemented by activating the controls of the car to act according to what the plan stipulates. This might mean that the accelerator control is commanded to increase the speed of the car. Or, the steering control is commanded to turn the steering wheel 30 degrees to the left or right.

One question arises as to whether or not the controls respond as they are commanded to do. In other words, suppose the AI has commanded the accelerator to increase, but for some reason it does not do so. Or, maybe it tries to do so, but the speed of the car does not increase. The controls activation feeds back into the virtual world model, and simultaneously the virtual world model is getting updated from the sensors, the sensor capture, and the sensor fusion. This allows the AI to ascertain what has taken place as a result of the controls being commanded to take some kind of action.

By the way, please keep in mind that though the diagram seems to have a linear progression to it, the reality is that these are all aspects of the self-driving car that are happening in parallel and simultaneously. The sensors are capturing data, meanwhile the sensor fusion is taking place, meanwhile the virtual model is being updated, meanwhile the system action plan is being formulated and reformulated, meanwhile the controls are being activated.

This is the same as a human being that is driving a car. They are eyeballing the road, meanwhile they are fusing in their mind the sights, sounds, etc., meanwhile their mind is updating their model of the world around them, meanwhile they are formulating an action plan of what to do, and meanwhile they are pushing their foot onto the pedals and steering the car. In the normal course of driving a car, you are doing all of these at once. I mention this so that when you look at the diagram, you will think of the boxes as processes that are all happening at the same time, and not as though only one happens and then the next.

They are shown diagrammatically in a simplistic manner to help comprehend what is taking place. You though should also realize that they are working in parallel and simultaneous with each other. This is a tough aspect in that the inter-element communications involve latency and other aspects that must be taken into account. There can be delays in one element updating and then sharing its latest status with other elements.

D-06: Automobile & CAN

Contemporary cars use various automotive electronics and a Controller Area Network (CAN) to serve as the components that underlie the driving aspects of a car. There are Electronic Control Units (ECU's) which control subsystems of the car, such as the engine, the brakes, the doors, the windows, and so on.

The elements D-01, D-02, D-03, D-04, D-05 are layered on top of the D-06, and must be aware of the nature of what the D-06 is able to do and not do.

D-07: In-Car Commands

Humans are going to be occupants in self-driving cars. In a Level 5 self-driving car, there must be some form of communication that takes place between the humans and the self-driving car. For example, I go into a self-driving car and tell it that I want to be driven over to Disneyland, and along the way I want to stop at In-and-Out Burger. The self-driving car now parses what I've said and tries to then establish a means to carry out my wishes.

In-car commands can happen at any time during a driving journey. Though my example was about an in-car command when I first got into my self-driving car, it could be that while the self-driving car is carrying out the journey that I change my mind. Perhaps after getting stuck in traffic, I tell the self-driving car to forget about getting the burgers and just head straight over to the theme park. The self-driving car needs to be alert to in-car commands throughout the journey.

D-08: V2X Communications

We will ultimately have self-driving cars communicating with each other, doing so via V2V (Vehicle-to-Vehicle) communications. We will also have self-driving cars that communicate with the roadways and other aspects of the transportation infrastructure, doing so via V2I (Vehicle-to-Infrastructure).

The variety of ways in which a self-driving car will be communicating with other cars and infrastructure is being called V2X, whereby the letter X means whatever else we identify as something that a car should or would want to communicate with. The V2X communications will be taking place simultaneous with everything else on the diagram, and those other elements will need to incorporate whatever it gleans from those V2X communications.

D-09: Deep Learning

The use of Deep Learning permeates all other aspects of the self-driving car. The AI of the self-driving car will be using deep learning to do a better job at the systems action plan, and at the controls activation, and at the sensor fusion, and so on.

Currently, the use of artificial neural networks is the most prevalent form of deep learning. Based on large swaths of data, the neural networks attempt to "learn" from the data and therefore direct the efforts of the self-driving car accordingly.

D-10: Tactical AI

Tactical AI is the element of dealing with the moment-to-moment driving of the self-driving car. Is the self-driving car staying in its lane of the freeway? Is the car responding appropriately to the controls commands? Are the sensory devices working?

For human drivers, the tactical equivalent can be seen when you watch a novice driver such as a teenager that is first driving. They are focused on the mechanics of the driving task, keeping their eye on the road while also trying to properly control the car.

D-11: Strategic AI

The Strategic AI aspects of a self-driving car are dealing with the larger picture of what the self-driving car is trying to do. If I had asked that the self-driving car take me to Disneyland, there is an overall journey map that needs to be kept and maintained.

There is an interaction between the Strategic AI and the Tactical AI. The Strategic AI is wanting to keep on the mission of the driving, while the Tactical AI is focused on the particulars underway in the driving effort. If the Tactical AI seems to wander away from the overarching mission, the Strategic AI wants to see why and get things back on track. If the Tactical AI realizes that there is something amiss on the self-driving car, it needs to alert the Strategic AI accordingly and have an adjustment to the overarching mission that is underway.

D-12: Self-Aware AI

Very few of the self-driving cars being developed are including a Self-Aware AI element, which we at the Cybernetic Self-Driving Car Institute believe is crucial to Level 5 self-driving cars.

The Self-Aware AI element is intended to watch over itself, in the sense that the AI is making sure that the AI is working as intended. Suppose you had a human driving a car, and they were starting to drive erratically. Hopefully, their own self-awareness would make them realize they themselves are driving poorly, such as perhaps starting to fall asleep after having been driving for hours on end. If you had a passenger in the car, they might be able to alert the driver if the driver is starting to do something amiss. This is exactly what the Self-Aware

AI element tries to do, it becomes the overseer of the AI, and tries to detect when the AI has become faulty or confused, and then find ways to overcome the issue.

D-13: Economic

The economic aspects of a self-driving car are not per se a technology aspect of a self-driving car, but the economics do indeed impact the nature of a self-driving car. For example, the cost of outfitting a self-driving car with every kind of possible sensory device is prohibitive, and so choices need to be made about which devices are used. And, for those sensory devices chosen, whether they would have a full set of features or a more limited set of features.

We are going to have self-driving cars that are at the low-end of a consumer cost point, and others at the high-end of a consumer cost point. You cannot expect that the self-driving car at the low-end is going to be as robust as the one at the high-end. I realize that many of the self-driving car pundits are acting as though all self-driving cars will be the same, but they won't be. Just like anything else, we are going to have self-driving cars that have a range of capabilities. Some will be better than others. Some will be safer than others. This is the way of the real-world, and so we need to be thinking about the economics aspects when considering the nature of self-driving cars.

D-14: Societal

This component encompasses the societal aspects of AI which also impacts the technology of self-driving cars. For example, the famous Trolley Problem involves what choices should a self-driving car make when faced with life-and-death matters. If the self-driving car is about to either hit a child standing in the roadway, or instead ram into a tree at the side of the road and possibly kill the humans in the self-driving car, which choice should be made?

We need to keep in mind the societal aspects will underlie the AI of the self-driving car. Whether we are aware of it explicitly or not, the AI will have embedded into it various societal assumptions.

D-15: Innovation

I included the notion of innovation into the framework because we can anticipate that whatever a self-driving car consists of, it will continue to be innovated over time. The self-driving cars coming out in the next several years will undoubtedly be different and less innovative than the versions that come out in ten years hence, and so on.

Framework Overall

For those of you that want to learn about self-driving cars, you can potentially pick a particular element and become specialized in that aspect. Some engineers are focusing on the sensory devices. Some engineers focus on the controls activation. And so on. There are specialties in each of the elements.

Researchers are likewise specializing in various aspects. For example, there are researchers that are using Deep Learning to see how best it can be used for sensor fusion. There are other researchers that are using Deep Learning to derive good System Action Plans. Some are studying how to develop AI for the Strategic aspects of the driving task, while others are focused on the Tactical aspects.

A well-prepared all-around software developer that is involved in self-driving cars should be familiar with all of the elements, at least to the degree that they know what each element does. This is important since whatever piece of the pie that the software developer works on, they need to be knowledgeable about what the other elements are doing.

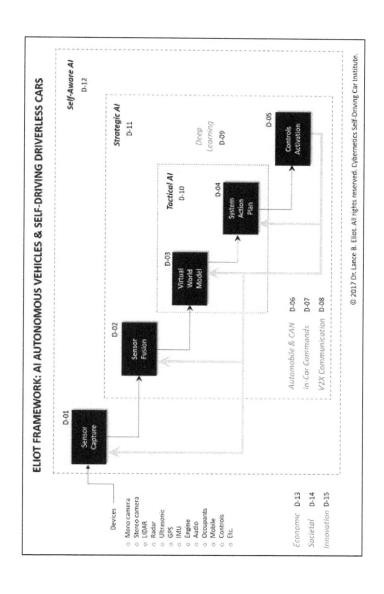

ELIOT FRAMEWORK: AI AUTONOMOUS VEHICLES & SELF-DRIVING DRIVERLESS CARS

Self-Aware AI
D-12

Strategic AI
D-11

Deep
Learning
D-09

Tactical AI
D-10

D-05
Controls
Activation

D-04
System
Action
Plan

D-03
Virtual
World
Model

D-02
Sensor
Fusion

D-01
Sensor
Capture

Devices
○ Mono camera
○ Stereo camera
○ LIDAR
○ Radar
○ Ultrasonic
○ GPS
○ IMU
○ Engine
○ Audio
○ Occupants
○ Mobile
○ Controls
○ Etc.

Automobile & CAN   D-06
In Car Commands   D-07
V2X Communication   D-08

Economic   D-13
Societal   D-14
Innovation D-15

CHAPTER 2
SOLVING LONELINESS
AND
AI SELF-DRIVING CARS

CHAPTER 2

SOLVING LONELINESS
AND AI SELF-DRIVING CARS

We are in the midst of a loneliness epidemic.

And, unfortunately, it is predicted to worsen.

According to stats by the U.S. Health Resources Services Administration (HRSA), one in five Americans indicates that they are lonely and feel socially isolated. Approximately 25% of Americans live alone. Loneliness is more than merely a debilitating state-of-mind, it also can be physically damaging and reportedly take months or years off your life span, increase your chances of having a stroke, along with being considered equal in body harm as if you were smoking 15 cigarettes per day.

By the demographics, those that are young tend to be vulnerable to loneliness, though we normally think only about the elderly being lonely (they are too, perhaps more obviously so). Many senior citizens find themselves single again, becoming widowed or suffering through a divorce, often having few friends, living by themselves, and gradually plunge into social isolation. Sadly, some become hermits, rarely leaving their adobe, succumbing to a vicious cycle of being alone and getting lonelier and lonelier over time.

You might assume that young people could not possibly be lonely since they are often armed with and have grown-up immersed in social media. Presumably, social media allows someone to have armies of friends, spread all across the globe, ready to befriend you at a moment's notice, twenty-four hours a day. The reality so far is that social media seems to have exacerbated loneliness.

Yes, that's right, social media appears to actually spur loneliness. How, you might wonder? It is believed that by substituting the in-person aspects of bonding and friendship with an electronic connection, social media access tends to make any friendship into an acquaintance rather than someone you'd consider as a heartwarming buddy.

Furthermore, there is a constant drumbeat on social media of wanting to showcase only the best side of your endeavors, creating a kind of competitiveness and one-upmanship. For various other paradoxically logical reasons, the vaunted hope of social media as a friend-generator seems to have underwhelmed expectations, and perhaps even fostered an adverse unexpected consequence of driving some into loneliness rather than away from it.

Sociologists have proposed that we all need to collectively combat loneliness, treating it like a disease or other scourge that requires overt action to cure. Non-profits and governmental programs have been springing up to attack the epidemic of loneliness, including offering tips and techniques to get past your loneliness and gain friendships, plus undertaking campaigns that increase awareness about loneliness and how to deal with it.

One of the toughest aspects is that loneliness tends to be viewed as a personal choice and therefore "live and let live" if that's what the person wants to do. Unfortunately, the stigma and falsehoods about loneliness are so infused into our culture and society that it is hard to get much support for trying to battle this plague.

Here's a proposal for you: Autonomous self-driving cars could help solve the loneliness epidemic.

The Role of Autonomous Cars In Solving Loneliness

I realize that it might seem like a humongous leap in reasoning to somehow connect the blight of loneliness to having autonomous self-driving cars serve as a kind of serum or antidote to solve the loneliness issue. Allow me a moment to explain why driverless cars a handy aid could be or at least possibly ameliorate the matter to some substantive degree.

First, let's be clear cut and agree that we don't yet have autonomous self-driving cars, meaning that we have not yet achieved true Level 5 driverless cars. There are various public roadway experiments and tryouts going on, usually involving having a human back-up driver in the self-driving car, and there is closed track or proving ground efforts too. But these are not fully autonomous cars, nor are they prevalent, and thus we don't really yet know what will happen once true autonomous cars are here and commonly available.

In my speeches at industry events, I've often likened this to questions about what will happen to humans when we are someday (presumably) colonizing Mars, assuming that we are able to construct rocket ships that can make such a voyage and that humans will want to go on these lengthy voyages. How will humans act while on a spaceship for these voyages and how will they act when living on another planet? We don't know for sure, and can only speculate, though it is reasoned speculation based on scientific and psychological research.

Let's try to use our scientific and psychological reasoning to infer how the advent of autonomous cars could battle loneliness.

There are several direct means and also indirect means.

Here they are:

• **Ridesharing Sharing.**

Autonomous cars are predicted to be a further boon to ridesharing, meaning that the ease of access to ridesharing will be greatly expanded. If that actually happens, it could allow for what some are calling Mobility as a Service (MaaS) and our society will be reshaped around the mobility afforded by driverless cars.

This could also mean that people might opt to rideshare together, more so than today, and thus you might encounter other people while ridesharing, gaining new friends, or being more face-to-face with existing friends or colleagues. It could chop away at the loneliness pillar.

• **Group Interaction Inside.**

Automakers are envisioning that autonomous cars will have a redesigned interior, no longer needing the steering wheel and driving controls. This frees up space inside a car. Concept designs suggest that you might have swivel seats and perhaps even a table to work on, allowing you to confer in a group setting while riding in an autonomous car.

Doing so would further cut a piece off of the loneliness megalith as people carry on meetings within an autonomous car.

• **Remote Group Interaction.**

Another possibility for the interior of autonomous cars involves having large LED screens on the windows, the screens facing inward, allowing you to enjoy say video streaming while a passenger in a driverless car.

With the widespread emergence of 5G as a speedy electronic communication protocol, you might opt to interact with others remotely, using the LED screens in a FaceTime or Skype manner, possibly to get some training or education courses undertaken while commuting. This same capability can allow someone that might be alone inside an autonomous car to interact with other people elsewhere. Take another notch off the loneliness stone.

• **Ease Of Transport.**

Currently, you need to find a human driver to take you someplace when you want to make use of a car. This can be difficult to arrange.

With an autonomous car, it is assumed that such cars will readily be available on an Uber or Lyft type of network, or possibly a Facebook or Twitter type of network, and you can easily request one to give you a lift. As such, the barrier to getting out of your home is lessened. It reduces the friction that nurtures loneliness.

• **AI Driver Can Be Your Friend.**

With advances in AI capabilities of Natural Language Processing (NLP) and socio-behavioral man-machine interaction, you'll likely be interacting fluently with the AI driving your autonomous car. Indeed, it is anticipated that such AI systems will incorporate empathetic computing that can gauge your emotions and respond to you in a seemingly emotion-based manner.

Your AI driving system might get to know you better than your human friends.

Each of those above aspects can be a separate means to mitigate loneliness. If you combine them together, you have an array of loneliness reducers that might be potent enough to make a dent in loneliness.

Conclusion

Does this all mean that autonomous cars are a guaranteed cure-all of human loneliness?

Decidedly, no.

Suppose the cost of using autonomous cars is high and therefore the assumed access to mobility is only for those that can afford it. This could leave out a large portion of society that is afflicted by loneliness.

Another concern is that the use of AI to bond with people might make humans actually less likely to seek out human relationships and human interactions. Why deal with the rough edges of humans, including getting into arguments and having tiffs, when you can chat with an AI system that treats you like royalty and never talks back. Anthropomorphizing of the AI could be another kind of scourge that we later on need to contend with.

I can tell you this much, it will be many years, likely decades, before we have autonomous driverless cars of a Level 5 that are pervasive in society. Keep in mind that we currently have over 250 million conventional cars in the United States alone and those are not going to overnight be transformed into driverless cars and nor be replaced overnight by driverless cars (the economics won't enable it).

So, let's be realistic and acknowledge that if autonomous cars are going to solve the loneliness epidemic, it's a remedy that won't be available for a long while to come. As such, meanwhile, we ought to be taking other prudent steps, and not waiting around until the driverless car as antidote arrives. Join the fight against loneliness, via more conventional approaches, and keep your eye on the future of autonomous cars.

CHAPTER 3
HEADLESS ISSUES
AND
AI SELF-DRIVING CARS

CHAPTER 3

HEADLESS ISSUES
AND
AI SELF-DRIVING CARS

I was in Boston for an industry conference and did a stare down with a driver that was barreling toward a crosswalk and seemed to not notice or perhaps not even care that I was walking across the street and doing so in the presumed safety of a clearly marked pedestrian crossing point.

The driver's eyes appeared to be aiming further down the block as though he was contemplating how he would contend with clogged traffic some fifty feet or more away from me, noticing a delivery truck that was double-parked and would partially block his passage once he got there.

Or, maybe he was pretending to not see me, in hopes that I would back away and retreat from my crossing, allowing him to proceed unimpeded for the moment.

It seems that different cities have differing rules-of-thumb about the eye-to-eye contact made between drivers and pedestrians.

In some cities, once eye contact is made, it usually means that one of the two will "win" and the driver for example will allow the pedestrian to cross, or vice versa. In other cities, making eye contact is the start of a war of eyebrow and eyeball expressing movements, trying to communicate silently about whether the driver has the right of the way or the pedestrian has the right of way.

Of course, per how I instructed my children when they were quite young, it is noteworthy that a car is ultimately going to prevail since it is a multi-ton vehicle that has deadly consequences once it strikes a pedestrian. My kids understood this notion and choose wisely to grant wide berth to approaching cars.

Meanwhile, on a daily basis, I see fully grown adults recklessly crossing streets and apparently believing that they are either made of pure steel and won't be harmed if rammed by a car, or they wander across effortlessly because they have some kind of Jedi mind trick to compel wayward drivers to stop in time.

Besides using our eyes, the act of communicating between driver and pedestrian can include arms, hands, sometimes fingers (well, one finger in particular), and yelling or shall I say vocalization.

Furthermore, these human body accoutrements can extend to driver-to-driver forms of communication too.

The other day, while I was driving in San Francisco, there was a driver that stuck his arm out his window and waved for me to go around him, since he was a ridesharing driver and was trying to stop in the street and have his passenger disembark. I had come upon his car and was patiently waiting behind him, unsure of what exactly the problem was, and took his waving action to mean that I could opt to navigate around him, assuming it was safe for me to do so.

This all brings up an interesting and very important question, namely what will happen once we have true self-driving cars that have no human sitting in the driver's seat?

You could say that the driverless car is headless, meaning there is not going to be a human head positioned near to the steering wheel and thus no one for you to do eye contact with. Nor would there be arms or hands or insulting fingers involved.

Let's unpack what the ramifications of the empty seat are and what can be done about it.

Getting Used To No Human In The Driver's Seat

I'll start with the aspect that it is eerie to see a car that doesn't have a driver seated behind the steering wheel.

Most of us tend to right away look at the driver of a car whenever we have a concern about where a car is headed. It is a natural inclination that we all have, based on years upon years of dealing with the antics and foibles of human drivers. Who is that person driving that car? What in the heck are they doing?

Right now, few of the autonomous cars being tried out on our public roadways are empty in the driver's seat because there is a human back-up driver in that position. In theory, the human back-up driver is only supposed to take the wheel when an emergent situation requires doing so, otherwise the human is merely monitoring the driving task and traffic conditions.

In any case, there is a human head there due to the back-up driver and thus it visually appears to be an everyday car because there is a human where we expect them to be.

If you went to a closed track or proving ground, you can watch as driverless cars make their way around faked streets and buildings, doing so without any human back-up driver. Upon witnessing a car that has no person in the driver's seat, you at first assume the car won't be going anywhere. Once the car gets underway, you have an immediate urge to protest and want to leap into the car to take over the wheel, based on the presumption that it is a runaway car.

Some jokesters have made online videos of them hiding inside a conventional car, modifying the driver's seat so that they can get inside of it and seemingly disappear from view, doing so to gauge the reaction of others that see the car driving down a street without any apparent human driver at the wheel. There are also bona fide scientists and researchers that have done something similar, often setting up remote driving controls or sitting in the backseat with a means to drive the car.

I bring up this aspect about the eeriness or spookiness to point out that it will likely take a while before we can all become comfortable with seeing a car in-motion on our public roadways that has no driver in the front position.

Assuming that driverless cars do indeed become proficient and safe enough to drive without a back-up human driver, we will gradually see these headless cars on a daily basis.

Eventually, no more double takes as you perchance see a driverless car going past you. No more lengthy mouth-gaping looks as you frantically try to discern whether there is a human driving the car (maybe there's a funster hiding!). The new norm will eventually become a sea of cars driving around us and they will not have a human head and nor human arms or any human at all in the driver's seat.

This might ultimately become even less obvious once the interiors of cars get rejiggered due to the advent of driverless cars.

Since there won't be a human driving position (some say), the car can have a completely different interior configuration than we have today. A popular redesign consists of swivel seats that are able to face each other, allowing four people to confer around a small table, and chat face-to-face while on a driving journey. Upon having a lot of cars on our roadways that have no driver's seat, it will lessen our tendency to gape and try to spot the presumed driver.

So, assuming we can inevitably overcome the shock of not seeing a driver, it nonetheless does not resolve the other more important concern consisting of communicating with a driver.

Communication With A Driver Is Vital

Pretend that a fully driverless car is coming down the street. You want to go into the crosswalk. You try to catch the eye of, well, nobody, since there isn't a human driver.

Sure, the self-driving car is equipped with cameras, and the AI system might be able to detect that you are gazing at the driverless car, but it has no immediate means of letting you know that you and it have made contact with each other.

One could argue that if the AI starts to slow down the car, this implies that the system saw you. Suppose though that the AI noticed a dog on the other side of the street and was slowing down because of the off-the-leash animal and hadn't noticed you at all. You'd have no immediate way of knowing that the AI was taking actions with the self-driving car because you and it had become copacetic.

Okay, maybe have the AI proceed to honk the horn of the car to confirm that it saw you making eye contact. Yikes! Imagine how noisy the world would become with a constant cacophony of horn honking. Plus, you still wouldn't know for sure whether the honking horn was intended for you or intended to scare-off the loose dog.

Realizing that having an empty spot for a driver is going to unsettle how we all communicate with the driver of a car, most of the automakers and tech firms are exploring alternative means to achieve similar functionality.

Here's the methods being tried:

- External displays on the driverless car
- V2V (vehicle-to-vehicle) electronic communications
- V2I (vehicle-to-infrastructure) electronic communications
- Robot-like device in the driver's position

One means to communicate with humans would be to have some kind of LED displays on the outside of the car. Thus, the AI system could flash a message or image on the display to provide a confirmation that it sees you or that depicts what driving action the AI is going to take.

This approach though raises as many questions as it answers.

If the electronic messages are too long, it might be difficult to read them or require so much time to comprehend that the display essentially fails to convey crucial indications to nearby humans on a timely basis. And, we need to ask, for which human is each message intended to reach, a notable problem if there are a multitude of pedestrians near to the driverless car.

Perhaps use emoticons. We've all gotten used to using emojis on our smartphones. It could be that via the use of similar at-a-glance visual icons there wouldn't be a need to display words or a narrative on the e-signboards of the autonomous car.

Meanwhile, there are some that are hoping to use the external surfaces of driverless cars to display electronic ads, possibly a handy money maker for the owner of the self-driving car. Unfortunately, you'd then have potentially the same displays that are supposed to be providing traffic and driving cues that are doing double-duty showcasing toothpaste ads. Confusing. Bewildering. Not a good double-duty.

Another approach involves mounting what appear to be giant eyeballs on the front hood of the car. The electronics makes the eyes seem like they are able to look at you, or look away, and seemingly act like a human's eyeballs would perform. This mimics what us humans are already used to seeing, though it omits the other means of conveying intent such as the waving of arms, hands, fingers, and vocalization.

Speaking of vocalization, some are trying out the use of audio speakers on the car so that it can seemingly talk to you. You've perhaps experienced this already on today's cars that have a security system installed, wherein if you walk too closely to the car, it emits a message such as stay back or keep away from the automobile.

Besides the displays and audio speakers, another approach involves electronic communication.

Driverless cars are aiming to use V2V that allows a car to essentially text a message to another car, allowing two or more cars to share messages with each other. This is going to become prevalent and expected for autonomous cars.

In addition, there will be V2P, consisting of the AI sending a message to a pedestrian, likely to their smartphone. Suppose you are waiting at a crosswalk. An approaching self-driving car could send a text message to your smartphone and signify that you can go ahead and cross the street.

For both the V2V and the V2P there are various drawbacks. We are going to have a mix of self-driving cars and human driven cars for quite a while, which means that the V2V won't be as effective in the case of communicating to a human driven car. The V2P obviously won't do so well if the humans nearby don't have a smartphone, or have one but it is switched-off, and so on.

The approach of using a robot-like head or upper body inside the self-driving car is considered by most to be gimmicky and unworkable.

The sci-fi looking robot would not be driving the car and instead only serve as a means of communicate with humans via its robotic eyeballs, arms, hands, and fingers. Think of this as a simplistic substitute for the body of a person. One downside is that it would use up space inside the car in the driver's position, though the robot device is not actually driving the car.

The other issue is whether it would be overly creepy and might dissuade the public from wanting to consider using self-driving cars.

Conclusion

I've often referred to this matter as the "head nod" problem and it is one of those vexing unsolved problems that will gradually impact the advent of self-driving cars.

Right now, there are so few driverless cars and they typically include a human back-up driver, all of which tends to mask or underplay the problem of how to communicate or signal to humans about what the AI system is intending to do.

Some pundits downplay the problem and seem to be unaware of how much of our daily lives involve making contact with human drivers, or at least using the human driver as a visual indicator of what a car is going to do next.

Whether you are a pedestrian or driving a car, there are expressive gestures and looks that keep our world from becoming an uncoordinated mess, akin to baseball players signaling each other about whether to leap off the base or take a swing at the next pitch. Without those subtle and yet telling and crucial communications, you can expect a lot of strikeouts and deadly losses on our roadways.

CHAPTER 4

ROAMING EMPTY
AND
AI SELF-DRIVING CARS

CHAPTER 4

ROAMING EMPTY AND
AI SELF-DRIVING CARS

Running a ridesharing or ride-hailing business these days is not for the faint of heart.

Both Uber and Lyft are infamous for losing money hand-over-fist, amounting to the tune of billions of dollars going down the drain.

One of the logistics aspects that can stymy these ride going services is the percentage of time that the passenger hauling car is empty of passengers.

Generally, a car being driven by an Uber or Lyft driver that is bereft of any passengers is not a good thing.

You can pretty much assume that when there isn't a passenger there also isn't any income being derived by the ridesharing effort. One quasi-exception consists of instances in which the driver is delivering something, perhaps a pizza or a burger or a package, and as such, there is presumably income covering the delivery action.

For purposes of simplicity, let's assume that delivering something is equivalent to having a passenger.

Thus, when I refer to an empty vehicle, it means that the car doesn't have a passenger and nor is it in the act of delivery. Also, for clarities sake, a passenger could be a human being, though the rider could also be a favored dog or cat that someone is paying for a breezy ride to the vet or to grandma's house.

Another factor to keep in mind about a so-called "empty vehicle" is that there is a human driver sitting in the driver's seat.

Sometimes it is confusing to refer to an empty car since it could imply that nobody is in the vehicle at all. In the context of ridesharing, an empty vehicle traditionally means that there is a driver and no one else in the vehicle.

I'll further point out that there might be a passenger in a car, but if they aren't paying anything to be there, they essentially count as an empty vehicle. Maybe a ridesharing driver decides to give a friend a free ride to the store, or perhaps the other person is a fellow driver that might be in training. If there's no dough derived from the passengers, it's considered an empty vehicle.

The formal wonky moniker is often referred to as the utilization component of ridesharing or e-hailing service, typically calculated as the percentage of time that a driver spends with a passenger. We can quibble a little bit about whether emptiness and utilization are the same or not, but for sake of discussion let's assume that they indeed are one and the same.

Industry Average Of Empty Car Time

Can you guess what the industrywide average of empty vehicle time is?

When I ask this question at conferences, attendees toss out all kinds of wild numbers.

Some think it must be rare that a ridesharing car is empty and so guess what it is maybe 1% or 2% of the time. Others guess that it might be relatively common to have an empty ridesharing car, and they guess that it might be the seemingly astronomical amount of say 20% or one-fifth of the time.

According to industry reported stats, the average time that a ridesharing vehicle is "empty" comes to about 41% of the time.

I hope that wasn't overly shocking for you (I should have said trigger alert).

Though the stats don't also say how much of that empty car time involves the car being in-motion, most would assert that the ridesharing cars are nearly always in motion when available to provide a ride.

Generally, when a ridesharing car is parked, it implies that the car is not available for a ride. There are exceptions, of course, but the gist is that the 41% implies that a significant chunk of the time that a ridesharing car is underway, it is empty.

The emptiness factor produces a lot of ugly and undesirable consequences.

A ridesharing car that 41% of the time is not earning money means that the cost of the driver and the cost of the car are having to be covered by the 59% of the time that a passenger exists.

Presumably, if you could decrease the emptiness, you could produce more income, and in theory pay, drivers more and more readily cover the costs of the car, along with gaining a profit.

Another aspect that gets people mad about the empty car phenomenon is that the vehicle is adding to traffic snarls, presumably exacerbated by the wasted 41% of the time there isn't a passenger in the car.

If you stand on the street corner of a busy city, you can likely see a parade of ridesharing cars after ridesharing cars that are cruising the streets, absent a passenger, and trolling or waiting for a passenger to hail the vehicle.

Anyone driving their car for their own purposes often gets steamed to see themselves surrounded by empty ridesharing cars. What might have taken ten minutes to drive from your office to a restaurant gets extended multifold by those darned empty ridesharing cars that are choking up traffic?

Cities have qualms too about the pollution that those empty cars are producing. It's one thing to be driving a passenger and producing pollution but driving an empty vehicle and gushing out pollutants seems especially egregious and foul.

An often-unstated downside of roaming empty cars is that presumably the risk of getting into a car crash or other incident is increased.

This risk is not due to the car being empty, but instead due to the length of time on the roadway and the distance traveled. The more any car is on the roadway, the chances of getting into an accident continue to be present.

Some question whether the safety compromise of having roaming ridesharing cars that are empty is warranted to the public at large, though few studies exist to predict how much of the 41% of that overall driving time is leading to car accidents (other than using generic driving stats as an approximation).

Recent Kerfuffle In NYC

A bit of a kerfuffle has arisen in New York City (NYC) on the emptiness conundrum.

The NYC Taxi and Limousine Commission (TLC) recently passed a new regulation that requires ridesharing firms in NYC to achieve a lowered rate of emptiness, reducing their average empty car time to 31% by August of next year (August 2020).

Nobody knows whether the 31% can be attained, nor exactly how to best reach it.

On the surface, aiming for a lessened emptiness factor is a good thing, though drivers are worried that it means they might be forced to cut back on their driving efforts and therefore earn less money, and the ridesharing services are concerned about backlash from all quarters.

For example, suppose that the time for you to wait once you've requested a ridesharing ride goes up, which could happen if the number of cruising empty cars is reduced to knock down the emptiness time.

As a customer, you aren't likely to be pleased that the emptiness factor went down and yet the delay for you to get a ride went up. All you'll care about is the wait time. Most ride-seeking people are bound to say that they don't care about emptiness and only care about getting a prompt ride.

You can argue that maybe their journey in the ridesharing car might be faster and they might end-up shell out less money for the ride once the emptiness rates drop to 31%, though right now that's a theoretical proposition and the actual impact could come out quite differently.

Uber has launched a lawsuit to overturn the new TLC rule, claiming in part that the rule was enacted without sufficient due diligence and that it was concocted by "a rushed and unlawful process, including reliance on flawed and arbitrary economic modeling, which was designed to arrive at a predetermined result that is likely not even feasible."

Oh, the web that does get weaved.

Here's an interesting point to consider: Will the advent of self-driving cars eliminate the emptiness factor, or will it be the same or perhaps even worse than with today's conventional cars?

Let's unpack the matter.

Self-Driving Cars And Ridesharing

True self-driving cars are ones that the AI drives the car entirely on its own and there isn't any human assistance during the driving task.

These driverless cars are considered a Level 4 and Level 5, while a car that requires a human driver to co-share the driving effort is usually considered at a Level 2 or Level 3. The cars that co-share the driving task are considered semi-autonomous, and typically contain a variety of automated add-ons that are referred to as ADAS (Advanced Driver-Assistance Systems).

There is not yet a true self-driving car at Level 5, which we don't yet even know if this will be possible to achieve, and nor how long it will take to get there.

Meanwhile, the Level 4 efforts are gradually trying to get some traction by undergoing very narrow and selective public roadway trials, though there is controversy over whether this testing should be allowed per se (we are all life-or-death guinea pigs in an experiment taking place on our highways and byways, some point out).

Since the semi-autonomous cars require a human driver, akin to any of today's conventional cars, I'm not going to consider the emptiness factor a Level 2 or Level 3 car (it would be the same as the emptiness of conventional cars).

Instead, let's focus on the emptiness or utilization aspects involving true self-driving cars, ones at Level 4 and Level 5.

Well, the first big difference is that when a true self-driving car is considered empty, it really is empty.

Recall that with conventional cars we were willing to say that a car was empty when there weren't any passengers, even though there was a human driver present.

Now, due to the AI driving system, there isn't a human driver and presumably not a provision allowing for a human driver (this is a controversial point, for which some believe that human driving ought to be still allowed in true self-driving cars).

From the perspective of a ridesharing or ride-hailing firm, removing the human driver is somewhat like a godsend. No more dealing with those darned human drivers that are cantankerous and complaining about the money they are making or being denied. Human drivers oftentimes pick and choose when they want to work and dare to take off days whenever they feel like it.

Overall, the headaches of human drivers are erased.

Furthermore, the AI driving system can drive whenever and wherever the owner of the self-driving car dictates. There are no debates about working late at night or having to drive to Timbuktu for fares. Instead, the owner deploys the self-driving car to any place and at any time.

Many are tempted to also say that the cost of the driver is removed. Yes, certainly the hourly fee paid to human drivers or commissions is no longer pertinent, but you need to impute the cost of the AI driving system as a kind of surrogate for the cost of a human driver.

The AI driving system consists of the plethora of sensors on the self-driving car, plus the computer processors, plus the AI software, and so on. The hardware is prone to wear-and-tear. The software will need updates.

All in all, there is still a form of "cost" associated with the driving act.

Nobody knows what the cost of these AI driving systems will be.

It will be interesting to see what happens when true self-driving cars start to compete head-to-head with human-driven ridesharing and ride-hailing cars. We will begin to know how the costs compare and whether the AI driving systems will indeed drive down the costs as most assume or hope will happen.

Self-Driving Cars And Emptiness

Returning to our focus on the topic of emptiness, there is nothing magical about self-driving cars that obviates the emptiness factor.

You can have self-driving cars roaming around and cruising the streets, doing so without passengers and in the same manner that human-driven "empty" ridesharing cars do so.

If that's the case, what do you predict the emptiness percentage will be?

It is tempting to say that it might be about the same as today's 41%.

Maybe, maybe not.

Some worry that it might be a lot higher.

Here's why that could happen.

Everyone that owns a true self-driving car is going to want to wring every dollar of ridesharing revenue they can out of the driverless vehicle. Might as well put the self-driving car into service nearly 24x7, minus the time needed to refuel or recharge the car, and minus the time needed for maintenance or repairs.

Imagine then a myriad, nay a swarm, consisting of hundreds or maybe thousands of self-driving cars roaming around, all waiting for that moment when they will be called into action to carry a passenger.

Furthermore, pundits keep saying that we can get rid of parking lots in downtown areas since the advent of self-driving cars will make parking lots no longer needed.

You would be stupid or at outright foolhardy to park your self-driving car when it could instead be picking up and transporting passengers.

At least that's the conventional wisdom about our future.

Some pundits are quick to gush about the fact that downtown areas will be able to reclaim parking lots for more important uses such as additional housing, or for businesses, or for retail space, or for greenspace and trees.

If you insist that parking ultimately is needed for those self-driving cars, the answer glibly stated is that parking in areas outside of downtown could be set up, doing so in places that the land is much cheaper and no humans live or want to live nearby.

Consider once again the emptiness factor.

You've got zillions of self-driving cars roaming around the streets of downtown, and for some percentage of the time, those self-driving cars are empty.

In addition, those self-driving cars are going to be driving empty to an outside area that has a parking lot. According to those pundits, no humans are going to be getting a lift out to those parking lots because the self-driving car parking space will be on the outskirts where no humans are desirous of the land.

When you start to add-up the emptiness time, it could be that self-driving cars will break the sound barrier of emptiness and reach astoundingly high percentages.

For those that own self-driving cars, the emptiness is going to hurt and could make the use of the self-driving car for ridesharing unpalatable.

Tackling The Emptiness

Ponder some of the adverse consequences already mentioned about emptiness and recast them into a world that includes true self-driving cars.

Here are some key points:

• The traffic snarls caused by self-driving cars vying for fares could be worse than what we already experience, partially due to the urgent need by the owners to seek out revenue to cover their expensive self-driving car purchases, and ongoing maintenance, and therefore sending their vehicles into an infinite search for paying riders.

• Human drivers that are also trying to drive, whether for ridesharing or personal purposes, are certainly going to get irked at seeing all those headless self-driving cars jamming up the streets. Might human drivers' rebel against their AI brethren?

• Passengers seeking a ride might have elongated wait times, especially if the predicted induced demand materializes (induced demand means that people today that don't use a car might be induced to do so, once we have self-driving cars).

• Journeys inside a self-driving car might be pleasant due to being able to relax and watch TV, but if the trip across town takes twice as long as it used to take, will riders be happy with the result?

• On a safety basis, once again the longer a car is in-motion and consuming miles, the risks of getting into a car accident continue unabated. Those that live in a Utopian world and insist that self-driving cars won't get into car accidents are making a false assumption that only self-driving cars will be on our roadways. We today have 250 million conventional cars in the United States alone and they aren't going away anytime soon, so stop pretending that we'll only have self-driving cars and realistically expect that we're going to have a mixture of human-driven cars and self-driving cars for a long time ahead.

• Pollution might be the one factor that does get impacted in a good way, namely that self-driving cars are likely to be Electrical Vehicles (EV), therefore the amount of pollution being pumped out of the cars will be less than today's gasoline-powered engines. The flip side to that coin is that there is a pollution footprint produced in the generation of electricity that is needed to recharge EVs.

Some say that we should restrict downtown areas to only self-driving cars and refuse to let human-driven cars into those areas.

In doing so, perhaps the emptiness factor might come down.

The logic being that if you have less of a supply of ridesharing vehicles in the restricted area, the demand is going to fill-up the self-driving cars more so. Of course, it might have the added effect of increasing wait times to get a ridesharing lift.

Will human-drivers be willing to get shoved down on the totem pole and sit on the outside while self-driving cars get the vaunted and exclusive access to making money in the steeped ridesharing locales such as a downtown area?

You can already see the ridesharing human drivers protesting that the small guy is getting the shaft, while the big businesses that own fleets of self-driving cars are getting outrageously wealthy.

Conclusion

I'm not trying to paint a doomsday picture concerning the role of self-driving cars.

My overall point is that some believe that the advent of self-driving cars will be a boon for mobility and make car rides readily accessible to all.

Though I am hopeful and optimistic about such an outcome, we need to realize that the real world is going to intrude on how things will play out.

Empty cars, whether for human drivers or for self-driving cars, do not provide a free lunch.

If a ridesharing car is not carrying a passenger or a package, presumably there is no one paying to have the resource meandering along on our streets.

Self-driving cars are a resource and have an associated cost.

Trying to figure out how to best manage that resource will be an issue for fleet owners and for individual owners, along with being an issue for cities and for people that simply want to get a ride.

It's going to be a challenge, and hopefully, one that we can avert the woe.

CHAPTER 5
MILLENNIALS EXODUS AND AI SELF-DRIVING CARS

CHAPTER 5

MILLENNIALS EXODUS AND AI SELF-DRIVING CARS

The latest stats indicate that millennials and Gen Z are continuing to exit from big U.S. cities, making this the fourth such year in a row of the mounting exodus.

Cities losing the largest numbers of young abandoners include New York City, Chicago, Houston, San Francisco, Las Vegas, and other marquee towns.

This movement out of big cities comes after there was a decade ago trend of youthful up-and-comers moving into city cores across the country, along with a seeming revitalization of downtown city areas to attract and retain young talent. You might recall that many heralded the rebirth of downtowns and assumed that the magnetic appeal would radiate endlessly.

Not so.

These latest adulting generations are now saying that they want out.

Why?

The most common reasons include:

- Unaffordable housing or inadequate housing

- Unsuitable place to start and raise a family

- Schools not good enough for a solid education for their kids

- Insufficient quality of life and downtrodden elements

Will the big cities be able to turnaround the trend and somehow attract back the millennials and Gen Z?

Though it would be nice to think that the cities would indeed clean-up their act, the odds are that they can't do so fast enough to stem the exodus. Plus, once matters like this get on a roll, it tends to be like the snowball careening out-of-control down a hill and getting more massive each passing year.

You might be wondering, where are these young adults going?

It seems that they are primarily relocating to nearby suburbs of the big city that they left, or they end up going to the suburbs adjacent to some other big city.

The rule-of-thumb appears to be that you ought to get out of the city itself yet be close enough to the city to leverage the advantages of city living.

Assuming that our future includes the emergence of true self-driving cars, it is useful to contemplate what the impact of driverless cars will have on the big city exodus matter.

My answer: Self-driving autonomous cars are going to accelerate and enable the exodus tenfold and spur nearly all generations (not just the youngest ones) toward living outside the big cities.

Let's unpack the assertion.

Levels Of Self-Driving Cars

First, I'll clarify what I mean when referring to true self-driving cars.

True self-driving cars are ones that the AI drives the car entirely on its own and there isn't any human assistance during the driving task.

These driverless cars are considered a Level 4 and Level 5, while a car that requires a human driver to co-share the driving effort is usually considered at a Level 2 or Level 3. The cars that co-share the driving task are described as being semi-autonomous, and typically contain a variety of automated add-ons that are referred to as ADAS (Advanced Driver-Assistance Systems).

There is not yet a true self-driving car at Level 5, which we don't yet even know if this will be possible to achieve, and nor how long it will take to get there.

Meanwhile, the Level 4 efforts are gradually trying to get some traction by undergoing very narrow and selective public roadway trials, though there is controversy over whether this testing should be allowed per se (we are all life-or-death guinea pigs in an experiment taking place on our highways and byways, some point out).

Since the semi-autonomous cars require a human driver, such cars aren't particularly important to the exodus question. There is essentially no difference between using a Level 2 or Level 3 versus a conventional car when it comes to the driving stress and strain.

It is notable to point out that in spite of those dolts that keep posting videos of themselves falling asleep at the wheel of a Level 2 or Level 3 car, do not be misled into believing that you can take away your attention from the driving task while driving a semi-autonomous car.

You are the responsible party for the driving actions of the car, regardless of how much automation might be tossed into a Level 2 or Level 3.

Let's then focus on the exodus impacts involving true self-driving cars, ones at Level 4 and Level 5.

Exodus Supported By Self-Driving Cars

A true self-driving car will contain only passengers and no human drivers.

Thus, for the estimated 70 billion hours of driving time that Americans consume each year in the United States currently, all those hours will be given back to those drivers as they become passengers rather than drivers.

Most experts agree that the capability of having an AI system undertake the driving for you will likely transform our society.

Suppose that today you commute to work, and it undermines your spirit and energy because you must drive in bumper to bumper traffic, contending with callous and nutty drivers around you. With self-driving cars, you let the AI deal with snarly traffic.

As a passenger, you can sit back and relax.

Maybe you listen to music or watch some TV while commuting to the office. Concept designs of self-driving cars include reclining seats or actual beds, allowing you to catch a nap while on-the-go.

It is anticipated that self-driving cars will have impressive network connections to allow passengers to stream video or undertake real-time remote interaction with others elsewhere. You can take a college class remotely, doing so as you spend time in your car.

Work will possibly be somewhat transformed due to the notion that you can work while doing your commute.

You can remotely connect to fellow workers in the office or bring together a global conference and video call with colleagues throughout the world. Meanwhile, the AI system is driving the autonomous car to whatever destination you've chosen.

If a big city lacks housing or has unaffordable housing, you normally would have to either sacrifice by finding some lousy housing option and endure it, or you would find a place outside the city but then deal with the commuter woes.

Since the commute is a crucial factor today, the odds are that you'd pick a living location that is close enough to the big city to minimize the commute, yet far enough away that you'd get the joys of living in a suburb.

The compromise of having to feel tethered to the big city due to the commute will gradually dissipate as self-driving cars become prevalent.

Imagine that someone lives forty-five minutes from the city and purposely selected their present apartment or house to keep their commute under an hour in length. Once true self-driving cars arise, the person might opt to move even further away, increasing their commute to say ninety minutes in length, yet they won't really feel an adverse difference in the elongated commute.

During the now hour and a half commute, the person can be doing work, they can be sleeping, they can even be remotely interacting with their kids at home, perhaps doing some double-checking on their homework that is due that day at school.

In short, self-driving cars will enable millennials and Gen Z to move further away from cities, extending the tether or connection without especially suffering the consequences.

Of course, if this kind of exodus is suitable for the younger generations, one might speculate that older generations could so the same thing. There's no magic about the younger generations wanting to live in nicer neighborhoods and be outside the ugliness of big cities, it's a proposition that appeals to all ages.

Constraints To The Exodus Path

The prediction that self-driving cars will enable and spur the exodus from big cities is quite compelling.

We do need to though consider potential constraints that might inhibit or disrupt the exit snowball.

First, we don't yet know what the cost of using a self-driving car will be.

If the per-mile cost is exorbitant, the tether to your big city job and living outside in the suburbs will once again involve a balancing act. The amount of money that you might save by finding less expensive housing in the suburb might be entirely consumed by the added cost of your self-driving car commute.

Second, we don't yet know when and how quickly self-driving cars will become prevalent.

Nobody can say for sure when true self-driving cars will arrive. Once they are here, they won't miraculously multiply overnight and suddenly replace all conventional cars.

It could be that self-driving cars are built and fielded in drips and drabs. This will affect the supply and demand aspects, which will thusly impact the availability and cost elements.

Perhaps self-driving cars are kept exclusively in the big cities since that's where the real money can be made. Those that own self-driving cars in fleets are going to want to maximize the money that they can make off the backs of the AI driving systems and those driverless cars.

Indeed, one likely downside of allowing a self-driving car to take you out to the suburbs is that once it gets there, the use of the self-driving car might not be as money-making in the suburban area, and perhaps the self-driving car has to drive back to the city, empty of passengers as it rushes back to the city to try and earn a buck.

Third, other factors might be more pronounced in the big city exodus than merely the advent of self-driving cars.

I've been focusing herein on the topic of how self-driving cars will shape the exodus movement, but driverless cars might be only one of numerous factors involved.

Some believe that the future of work will involve workers not having to come to an office anymore. You can live in the suburbs and telecommute to work, doing so via fast networks and computers at home.

There might not be a need to come to a big city, at least for work purposes, and instead, you might go to the big city on occasion to enjoy a play at a major theatre or various big city activities and nightlife.

The use of a driverless car might only marginally be a crucial reason for an exodus to the suburbs. Sure, self-driving cars could presumably make it easier to go to the big city when you felt like it, but the driverless car wouldn't be an instigator or promoter per se of the exodus enabling aspects.

Conclusion

I might have whetted your appetite for packing up your big-city apartment and heading out to the suburbs.

Don't start packing just yet if your decision to make the move is based on the expectation that you'll have available true self-driving cars.

The odds are that the upcoming even younger generations, younger than the millennials and Gen Z, those generations will have the greater opportunity to consider leveraging self-driving cars in choosing where they live.

For most of today's millennials and Gen Z, there might be spotty chances of being able to take advantage of self-driving cars, though their children will be more likely the beneficiaries of driverless cars.

Whichever generation is around when true self-driving cars hit the road, it is relatively safe to say that the use of self-driving cars will open doors to longer travel times being amenable and tolerable, allowing people to go greater distances for whatever reasons they wish to do so.

Leave the driving to the AI, laugh at the commute woes, and don't let the travel times overly hamper your decisions about where you live versus where you work.

CHAPTER 6

RECESSION WORRIES AND AI SELF-DRIVING CARS

CHAPTER 6
RECESSION WORRIES AND
AI SELF-DRIVING CARS

The media is doing a lot of handwringing about whether the U.S. economy is heading toward a recession.

Some analysts point to signs such as inverted yield curves and other economic metrics that look as though they are weakening toward doomsday.

The formal definition of a recession is that once we've suffered through two consecutive quarters of negative growth in the GDP (Gross Domestic Product), we are smack dab in a recession.

The oft-quoted joke about the difference between being in a recession versus a depression is that if you get laid-off from your job, it's a depression, while if your neighbor gets laid-off, it's a recession. Either way, it's bad times and something we'd all likely hope to avoid.

One concern is that we might be able to talk ourselves into a recession.

The psyche of businesses and consumers is crucial to whether a recession can take hold. When there's a constant drumbeat of handwringing about a recession, it can prod everyone into taking pre-recession protective measures.

The act of performing pre-recession protective measures can serve to stoke the embers of a recession into becoming a full-fledged recession.

You could say that we can produce our own self-fulfilling prophecy.

We all thought we were going to get mired into a recession, and so we allowed ourselves to go that route. Voila, we were right (though wrongheaded since we carelessly pushed our own way into the recession).

Here's a key point to consider: The pre-recession anticipatory moves are going to sink true self-driving cars, whether we even get into a full-blown recession or not.

Let's unpack the matter.

Defining Self-Driving Cars

It is important to clarify what I mean when referring to true self-driving cars.

True self-driving cars are ones that the AI drives the car entirely on its own and there isn't any human assistance during the driving task.

These driverless cars are considered a Level 4 and Level 5, while a car that requires a human driver to co-share the driving effort is usually considered at a Level 2 or Level 3. The cars that co-share the driving task are described as being semi-autonomous, and typically contain a variety of automated add-ons that are referred to as ADAS (Advanced Driver-Assistance Systems).

There is not yet a true self-driving car at Level 5, which we don't yet even know if this will be possible to achieve, and nor how long it will take to get there.

Meanwhile, the Level 4 efforts are gradually trying to get some traction by undergoing very narrow and selective public roadway trials, though there is controversy over whether this testing should be allowed per se (we are all life-or-death guinea pigs in an experiment taking place on our highways and byways, some point out).

Since the semi-autonomous cars require a human driver, such cars aren't particularly important to the exodus question. There is essentially no difference between using a Level 2 or Level 3 versus a conventional car when it comes to the driving stress and strain.

It is notable to point out that in spite of those dimwits that keep posting videos of themselves falling asleep at the wheel of a Level 2 or Level 3 car, do not be misled into believing that you can take away your attention from the driving task while driving a semi-autonomous car.

You are the responsible party for the driving actions of the car, regardless of how much automation might be tossed into a Level 2 or Level 3.

Overall, the pre-recession preparations will do the most damage to the progress on true self-driving cars, while simultaneously likely helping the semi-autonomous cars to a limited extent.

The rationale for this assertion is made next.

Recession Impacts On Business

There is a myriad of ways in which a recession impacts business.

During the pre-recession anticipatory phase, businesses start to take proactive actions that are baby steps toward what they willfully do once a recession occurs.

Consider the baby steps that some automakers and tech firms are on the verge of undertaking, or that in their vaunted boardrooms they are discussing in a quite distraught manner:

- Stop Or Slow Down Speculative Efforts. Businesses prefer a sure thing rather than speculative bets if a recession is coming. True self-driving cars are a speculative bet. Nobody can say when they will be achieved, and nor whether society is going to readily accept driverless cars. Executives that staunchly believe a recession is coming are open to temporarily stopping their true self-driving car efforts or slowing down what is taking place (depending upon the perceived strategic value of their driverless car initiatives and the progress made to-date).

- Cut costs. Getting ready for a recession is like getting ready for a rainy day, a very rainy day that might last for a long time. The most obvious preparation involves cutting costs. You must assume that revenue is likely to drop during a recession, so self-preservation means chopping out costs. The effort to design, build, test, and field a self-driving car is pricey. You can certainly try to cut costs, but the odds are that it will disrupt the driverless car development and elongate the path to achieving self-driving cars.

- Outside Financing Dries Up. The millions upon millions and into the billions of dollars needed to arrive at a true self-driving car are oftentimes being partially funded using financial instruments, rather than solely on internal funding. Unfortunately, the outside money is bound to dry up if a recession is seen as imminent. Like the famous line that if there's no bucks, there's no Buck Rogers, when there's no money, there's no driverless cars getting onto the streets.

- Justification Becomes Stringent. Projects at large firms tend to require a self-contained ROI (Return On Investment) once a recession is looming. Whereas during the good times a risky project would be fine and if it tanked the cost could be recouped by some other more profitable projects, the recession flag changes internal procedures to seek out only efforts that can showcase they will bring in the dough. True self-driving cars are hoped to make tons of money, but nobody knows if they will. So, driverless car projects can't likely meet the pay-your-own-way criteria.

- Short-term Overtake Long-Term. Though there is a lot of hue and cry about publicly traded firms being preoccupied with their quarterly results, due to the marketplace reactions at each quarterly report, nonetheless savvy executives try to have both a short-term and long-term perspective. Once a recession strikes, being long-term focused gets squeezed. Do what you need to do to survive in the short-term, and later revisit the long-term. Generally, self-driving cars are a long-term play, not a short-term aspect, thus the driverless car will get reduced in priority during a recessionary climate.

- Downsize Your Workforce. Laying off people is a fast way to reduce costs and lighten up for a recession. For self-driving cars, it takes gobs of highly specialized and expert AI developers and teams to develop the hardware and especially the software for self-driving tech. Once you start laying off that kind of talent, the odds are that the remaining labor will be disrupted, and gaps will be left in their skillsets. They won't be able to push ahead as quickly on the company driverless car efforts, nor will they be able to do the full range of what is required.

- Quality Gets Usurped. One of the subtle and yet frightening actions that firms sometimes take is to sacrifice on quality to get ready for a recession. Suppose you are testing your self-driving cars, doing so extensively and at a great cost. You could convince yourself that all that testing isn't necessary and sharply reduce it. This might at first seem helpful, but the lessened testing might ultimately lead to driverless car crashes and untoward incidents, knocking out the self-driving car aim and getting the firm into scalding hot water.

•   Get Something Out-The-Door. If your self-driving car efforts have been relatively quiet and discreet, the marketplace might perceive that you are draining resources with no tangible results. As such, when a recession is on the horizon, there is a temptation to shove out-the-door whatever driverless car you've got. Putting it onto the roadways will spotlight that you are presumably making solid progress. The key problem though is whether the self-driving car is ready for prime time and if not then it could be endangering us all.

There are more steps that businesses can take to prepare for a recession, but the list herein gives you a flavor for what might be undertaken.

Conclusion

Since true self-driving cars are the furthest to reaching fruition, the "next best thing" involves tossing your Level 4 and Level 5 efforts toward the Level 2 and Level 3 systems, assuming that you are embarking on the full range from Level 2 to Level 5.

In essence, you can rob Peter to pay Paul, shifting the resources and attention away from your autonomous cars to the semi-autonomous ones.

Why?

The semi-autonomous cars are already in the marketplace and are continuing to come into the marketplace. Therefore, any self-driving tech that is sitting on a futuristic self-driving car might be a candidate to place into a semi-autonomous car that will be sold to consumers tomorrow.

The recessionary mindset means that you are tempted to take away from a speculative effort and give to something that will be able to turn a buck sooner.

Unfortunately, it isn't as easy as it might seem to shift from the autonomous automation into the semi-autonomous realm. Furthermore, the talent working on the autonomous systems will potentially get distraught at having to "downgrade" to semi-autonomous systems, meaning they'll likely bolt to some other firm that is keeping their eye on true driverless cars.

In any case, I don't want to urge anyone to be taking pre-recession protective measures, and particularly when it comes to the moonshot goal of achieving self-driving cars.

Do not interpret my remarks as a prod toward making a recession come to reality.

In fact, if you are finding yourself falling into the trap of accidentally starting to act as though a recession is coming, perhaps my remarks will get you to rethink your actions.

Say it with me, there isn't a recession forthcoming and we aren't going to let ourselves incite one by having negative thoughts.

Switch over to some positive karma instead.

There might be a rough spot when self-driving cars are first becoming viable, during which there might be only wealthy related owners, almost like trying to be the first into a hot IPO, but once that era passes, I believe that the mobility-for-the-few will transform into the mobility-for-the-all.

Maybe I'm optimistic, and if so, I'm happy that I am.

CHAPTER 7

REMOTE OPERATIONS ISSUES AND AI SELF-DRIVING CARS

CHAPTER 7

REMOTE OPERATIONS ISSUES AND AI SELF-DRIVING CARS

At the TechCrunch Disrupt conference in San Francisco on October 3, 2019, one of the most interesting panel sessions about the future of mobility brought together Jesse Levinson, co-founder of Zoox, along with Manik Gupta, Chief Product Officer at Uber, and Sebastian Thrun, co-founder of Udacity and keenly focused these nowadays on his newest role as the CEO at Kitty Hawk (aiming to bring flying cars to reality).

One of the points by Jesse was like hitting the proverbial nail on the head, and for which I chatted with him after the panel to acknowledge his remark, namely this: Wireless should not be a safety case for self-driving cars.

Many would let this insightful remark roll in one ear and come out the other side, not necessarily realizing the gravity of its proclamation.

As background, there are some in the driverless car industry that are touting their use of teleoperations to aid in so-called self-driving car advancements. This means that when a self-driving car gets stuck in some manner such as confused when reaching a roadway construction site, it will "phone home" by activating a communications link to a human operator.

The human operator might be anywhere on planet Earth, perhaps just miles from the bewildered driverless car or the operator might be sitting in a dark room on the other side of the globe, ready to take over the driving task from the on-board AI system that was driving the vehicle.

Though at first glance it might seem like having a human "driver" as a remote back-up makes sense, you need to carefully consider the ramifications of such a strategy.

As per the sentiment of Jesse's remark, betting on a wireless connection for the safety of a self-driving car and its human occupants, and likewise the lives of those nearby the driverless car doesn't seem like an appropriate approach to many.

Indeed, it is downright dangerous when used as a crutch in any safety-related real-time on-demand urgency of a true self-driving car.

Let's unpack the matter.

Self-Driving Car Levels

It is important to clarify what I mean when referring to true self-driving cars.

True self-driving cars are ones that the AI drives the car entirely on its own and there isn't any human assistance during the driving task.

These driverless cars are considered a Level 4 and Level 5, while a car that requires a human driver to co-share the driving effort is usually considered at a Level 2 or Level 3. The cars that co-share the driving task are described as being semi-autonomous, and typically contain a variety of automated add-ons that are referred to as ADAS (Advanced Driver-Assistance Systems).

There is not yet a true self-driving car at Level 5, which we don't yet even know if this will be possible to achieve, and nor how long it will take to get there.

Meanwhile, the Level 4 efforts are gradually trying to get some traction by undergoing very narrow and selective public roadway trials, though there is controversy over whether this testing should be allowed per se (we are all life-or-death guinea pigs in an experiment taking place on our highways and byways, some point out).

Since the semi-autonomous cars require a human driver, such cars aren't particularly pertinent to the teleoperation question.

Most would concede that the human driver will be physically present in the vehicle for any Level 2 and Level 3 car. Thus, having a connection to a remote driver would be rather unusual and seemingly unnecessary (unless you believe that the in-car driver might have suffered a heart attack or otherwise falter in the driving task).

In most jurisdictions, the driver sitting in the driver's seat is considered the responsible party for the driving actions of the car. It is notable to point out that in spite of those dumbbells that keep posting videos of themselves falling asleep at the wheel of a Level 2 or Level 3 car, do not be misled into believing that you can take away your attention from the driving task while driving a semi-autonomous car.

Remote Operations Aspects

For remote driving of a car, the mainstay of the focus involves Level 4 and Level 5 driverless vehicles.

Some liken the concept of a remote operator for Earth-bound driverless cars to the notion of landing a rover on Mars and being able to remotely operate the rover.

If we can remotely control a vehicle that's all the way on Mars at 140 million miles distant from us, and presumably be able to adroitly drive around on the unforgiving Martian landscape, certainly we can do the same for a driverless car that's just a few hundred miles or maybe several thousand miles away here on Earth.

The faulty logic in the analogy to a Mars rover is that if you were to consult with any versed space scientists and engineers, you'd realize that they aren't betting on a tightly woven and fully assured remote connection occurring in real-time per se.

Problematic aspects can readily arise, including:

- The connection can have delays or latency

- The connection can be intermittent

- The connection can fail completely

- The connection can have noise and be unintelligible

- The connection can be fraudulently overtaken

- Etc.

I realize that the vast distance to Mars tends to exacerbate these connection woes, but don't be fooled into thinking that those same issues cannot arise when the distance is just hundreds or thousands of miles away.

When safety comes to play, any reliance on a remote operator means that you are willing to increase your risks that the remote operation will not be able to occur on a timely basis.

Suppose a self-driving car comes upon a construction zone and gets overwhelmed by a slew of cones and a construction crew that is meandering around.

Handing over the driving controls to a remote human operator seems like a clever and bona fide means to handle the situation.

Imagine though that the remote human operator instructs the car to proceed ahead, doing so under the watchful eye of the faraway driver.

Suddenly, the connection drops.

What happens next?

Maybe the driverless car should continue ahead since that was the last instruction is received. Of course, if the car is about to fall into a gaping hole in the road, we probably wouldn't want the vehicle to blindly proceed on its own.

You might be tempted to say that it is obvious that if the connection is broken then the driverless car should immediately come to a halt. Unfortunately, there are plenty of circumstances whereby halting the car can lead to other consequential dangers, such as being stranded now in the middle of a road or sitting in a place that other vehicles might ram into the stuck car.

Overall, a remote operator could inadvertently cause a driverless car to get itself into a worsened posture than if the AI was tending to its own affairs.

And, purists would assert that a true self-driving car is one that has no human driving at all, for which the use of a remote operator violates that, rule.

There is a subtle and potent urge to have a human driver potentially be at-the-ready to jump into the midst of a driving task that an AI system is supposed to be doing. You might think of this as a parent that is aiding their teenage driver learning how to drive. The parent is willing to reach over and take the wheel since they are being sincere in their desire to aid their child.

One concern is that we aren't going to arrive at true self-driving cars if we bake into the equation a human driver. Sure, the human driver isn't sitting inside the car, but nonetheless, you are saying that at some point the AI can't cut it and therefore a human driver is needed.

Will your teenage ever really be able to drive a car on their own, if they rely upon the parent sitting nearby to take over the controls?

In the case of a driverless car, would a driverless car that requires a remote human operator be properly referred to as a driverless car, though it apparently needs a human driver from time-to-time?

Many would assert that it is not a true self-driving car and merely another kind of semi-autonomous car.

Remote Operators Aspects

As mentioned, there are lots of potential connection disruptions and issues that can impede a real-time effort to drive a vehicle remotely.

You also need to consider the nature of the remote human operator as another risk factor.

In theory, the human remote operator will be instantly available and will be remarkably aware and astute whenever a driverless car needs help.

You cannot say for sure that any of those facets will always occur.

Perhaps there is a delay in notifying the remote human operator, thus losing precious seconds when the touch of a human driver is apparently required.

Maybe the human remote operator is distracted by some other task, perhaps already engaged in aiding another driverless car that has requested assistance.

Even if the human operator is attentive and alert, they still are reliant on whatever the driverless car is showing them about the driving environment. The cameras might be obscured, or other sensors might be reporting data insufficiently for the remote operator to get a comprehensive understanding of the driving scene.

There might also be a remote human operator that has received inadequate training and perhaps has been working a 12-hour shift. They are worn out and won't be remotely operating your car as carefully as you might so wish.

If you were a passenger inside a car that had a remote human operator, how safe would you feel about the matter?

At least when you are in an Uber or Lyft, you can see the driver with your own eyes.

You can assess the aptitude and awareness of the driver.

You are obviously still dependent upon the driver, but at least you can have a greater assurance of the driver's capabilities and attention to the driving task (some argue that a driverless car being piloted by a remote operator could have a camera pointed at the remote operator, thereby providing a semblance of having the driver sitting in the car, though this has its own downsides and complications).

From a safety perspective, the remote human operator presents at least three key safety gaps:

- Risks of connection or networking disrupts and latencies during the driving task

- Risks of the human operator not being attentive to the driving task

- Risks of the driving environment not being well-conveyed to the remote human operator

Other Remote Connections

One of the most frequent assumptions that many have about self-driving cars is that these autonomous cars will be immersed in all kinds of connected communications.

There are V2V (vehicle-to-vehicle) electronic communications that will allow a self-driving car to communicate with other self-driving cars. This might involve alerting that there is debris on the roadway and thus one self-driving car that comes upon the matter will notify upcoming driverless cars to be watchful.

There could be V2I (vehicle-to-infrastructure) electronic communications. Roadway infrastructure such as bridges might send out a signal to forewarn driverless cars that the bridge is unpassable.

There is OTA (Over-The-Air) electronic communications, meaning that a driverless car can send its data up to the cloud and also receive software patches and updates from the cloud.

Since those capabilities also depend upon making remote connections, you would be right in believing that a true self-driving car should not be reliant upon any of those added features during the performance of the driving task in real-time.

A true self-driving car should be able to conduct the driving task without the need for V2V, without the need for V2I, and without the need for OTA.

Don't misunderstand that statement.

I'm not saying that self-driving cars should eschew the use of V2V, V2I, or OTA.

Instead, the point is that those should not be safety-critical elements. The safety of the self-driving car must not depend upon the expectation that a reliable and robust connection to V2V, V2I, or OTA is available.

The goal is a fully standalone self-driving car.

A human driver can drive a car without any kind of remote connection. You can get into a car and drive it without having a cell phone. You can drive it on a fully standalone basis.

True self-driving cars are supposed to be able to drive a car in any manner that a human driver could drive a car (some exceptions apply).

Pundits of self-driving cars might argue that a driverless car needs at least one kind of remote connection, namely the use of GPS to be able to navigate while driving.

Well, you might recall that human drivers once drove cars without GPS.

Presumably, a true self-driving car should be able to drive even without a GPS, or when a GPS is having remote connection issues. Many would say that the use of on-board stored maps and in combination with the IMU of the car should suffice when needed (in a pinch).

Conclusion

There is a myriad of variants on the remote operator matter.

For example, some agree that remote operators should not be a safety case but can be allowed for other kinds of use cases of self-driving cars.

Suppose you have self-driving cars in a parking lot that has no people in it. There aren't any humans in the cars, and there aren't any humans in the restricted parking lot. Since there aren't any humans that might get hurt, perhaps its okay to allow remote operators to control the self-driving cars.

The worst-case scenario is that a car bumps into another car.

One concern about allowing any kind of remote operation is that it might be invoked in situations whereby there are humans that could get hurt. Imagine that a human inadvertently wanders into the restricted parking lot, or a human was asleep in one of the parked cars and was not noticed. And so on.

A more everyday example would be a remote dispatcher that connects to a self-driving car and indicates a destination. The remote dispatcher is not a remote operator or driver. Instead, the remote dispatcher only provides overall directives and it is then entirely up to the on-board AI to drive the car.

Another viewpoint is that maybe we consider using human remote operators temporarily, allowing us to start using self-driving cars right away, and once self-driving cars are fully readied then we revoke the remote operations capability.

Here's another angle on allowing remote human operators that might pique your interest.

There are conspiracy theorists that are worried that AI systems will take over all our cars, making us reliant on AI and becoming essentially enslaved to AI. In that use case, the relief valve is that there would be human operators that could take control of the AI-slave cars and save us from utter domination and destruction.

Overall, the remote operation of self-driving cars is a controversial topic and there are vigorous debates and disagreements involved.

Some companies are betting that remote operators for driving will become a booming business.

They are readying offices that will house dozens or even hundreds of remote drivers. The locations are dispersed around the world so that a 24 x 7 human driving remote operator will be available at any time of the day or night.

An autonomous car is presumably autonomous, or can we have autonomous cars that are also able to use remote human operators?

Yes, some point out, human remote operators can be established, and we can use them if we realize the safety risks involved and are willing to accept those risks.

For those of you that believe the AI will be safer, you would be alarmed that we are introducing humans into the loop.

If you believe that the AI won't be safe enough, perhaps keeping humans in the loop will help, though it could also hurt.

Can we use remote operators as an armchair driver, co-sharing the driving task with the AI, allowing the AI to deal with the moment-to-moment driving and then having the remote human deal with less time-dependent facets?

There are lots of combinations and permutations to be resolved, and the safety of us all is at stake.

CHAPTER 8

BOOMERANG KIDS

AND

AI SELF-DRIVING CARS

CHAPTER 8

BOOMERANG KIDS

AND

AI SELF-DRIVING CARS

They call them boomerang kids.

The word "kids" is rather misleading since the ages involved are typically young adults, so substitute the notion of kids (i.e., toddlers to teenagers) to instead mean offspring as in your kids that you faithfully raised and sent out into the harsh real-world.

For the boomerang aspects, it's a clever metaphorical device that suggests a situation or aspect wherein you toss something into the air, and it manages to come back to you.

Based on those mindful delineations of the popular phrase, we can now put it all together and state that a boomerang kid is an offspring that though initially cast into the real-world then returns home to the nest.

When a parent drops off their son or daughter at college, the occasion was especially momentous because the conveyor belt of life was going to have their loved one get a college degree and then take a job, essentially meaning that coming home to roost would never happen again. Sure, you might see them during semester breaks and perhaps temporarily host them over their college summers, but you knew that upon college graduation they were gone for good.

Instead, the latest trend is that you end-up with them moving back into your home post-college and they are there to stay for possibly quite a while.

Some estimates suggest that perhaps 15%-20% of millennials aged 25 to 35 are now living at home with their parents.

That's nearly one-fifth of all millennials, a staggering number that is delaying the presumably inevitable act of moving out and living on their own.

What gives?

Here are some of the key reasons cited for the trend:

Onerous Student Debt. Nationally, there is about $34,000 in average outstanding debt for every millennial that went to college. Ouch! That is a huge debt load for someone just beginning their career. Meager starting salaries will barely cover the debt payments, let alone also cover the costs of living on their own.

Exorbitant Housing Costs. Paying the rent is tougher than it used to be. In many major cities, the cost to get an apartment has risen precipitously and what you can afford is often in destitute areas. Would you rather that your offspring lived in a high-risk high-crime downbeat area, or have them at home? Our natural protective mechanism says let them come home.

Not Ready For Adulting. Critics argue that baby boomers have done a lousy job at preparing millennials and Gen Z for becoming adults. Maybe the codling when the kids were kids made them soft for being able to navigate day-to-day real-world tasks. The so-called "helicopter parenting" by parents that did everything for their children seems to have backfired by rendering those youths ultimately ill-prepared for living as independent adults.

Ramp-Up Time Needed. Some assert that the post-college years now have to include a ramp-up period, whereby rather than immediately stepping out on your own, you use time at home to get your act together, including saving up money so that you can truly make the jump into independent living. There's a newly inserted life-buffer that must exist between the end of college and the start of your own journey as a full adult.

Much of the media coverage of the boomerang kids tends to imply that these young adults are lazy, unwilling to tackle the real world, and are merely heading home because it's the easiest and least demanding way to live.

I'm not going to entertain that overreaching smear.

Of course, there are some millennials that might well fit into that castigated category. I'd bet though that by-and-large most of the post-college youths would prefer to be on their own and not staying at home if they could reasonably swing doing so.

It's also important to acknowledge that there is a portion of these boomerang kids that come home to help take care of their parents. For those angelic young adults, you've got to hand it to them, namely, they are often delaying their own opportunities as independent adults to care for a parent that might be elderly or infirm. Please don't place those types of boomerang kids into the same category as the ones that are coming home because they have no gumption or spirit to do things on their own.

Advice offered to parents that have boomerang kids living with them on a post-college basis is to try and adroitly find ways to guide the young adults toward gradually moving out.

If you don't do something constructive to help nudge the boomerang kids, they might stay longer than is needed and likely longer than is good for them and you.

There's a crass statement that you can end-up with barnacles that won't ever shake-off.

Particularly worrisome are the parents that seem to trap their boomerang kids into staying at home, doing so by neglecting to provide outward progression steps, yet at the same time, those parents will often loudly decry that their son or daughter is still living at home. Talking via both sides of your mouth is unseemly and will inexorably destroy the relationship between you and your offspring.

Some believe that the parent should work with their boomerang kid to establish a personal budget, getting the son or daughter to learn about taking care of their own financial affairs.

Another idea is to have the offspring pay "rent" while at home, perhaps doing so by earned "points" when doing chores (akin to a kids allowance), or taken out of whatever monies they might be making at their first job (but charging less than the more burdensome real rents if they had their own apartment).

You could even use the rent payment as a form of accumulation for when they opt to move out. In other words, once the boomerang kid moves out of the house, you hand them a check for the total amount of "rent" that they paid while staying at home. This then conveniently becomes a means to have the offspring build a bit of a nest egg and fosters a launching pad for living on their own.

Here's an interesting twist to consider: What will happen to boomerang kids in an era of true self-driving cars?

My theory is that the advent of self-driving cars will enable the boomerang kids to bounce out of the home sooner than they are doing so today.

I don't think that the phenomena of boomerang kids will be expunged, but it will be substantively impacted and in a manner that will tend to benefit the stakeholders involved.

Let's unpack the matter.

The Levels Of Self-Driving Cars

It is important to clarify what I mean when referring to true self-driving cars.

True self-driving cars are ones that the AI drives the car entirely on its own and there isn't any human assistance during the driving task.

These driverless cars are considered a Level 4 and Level 5, while a car that requires a human driver to co-share the driving effort is usually considered at a Level 2 or Level 3. The cars that co-share the driving task are described as being semi-autonomous, and typically contain a variety of automated add-ons that are referred to as ADAS (Advanced Driver-Assistance Systems).

There is not yet a true self-driving car at Level 5, which we don't yet even know if this will be possible to achieve, and nor how long it will take to get there.

Meanwhile, the Level 4 efforts are gradually trying to get some traction by undergoing very narrow and selective public roadway trials, though there is controversy over whether this testing should be allowed per se (we are all life-or-death guinea pigs in an experiment taking place on our highways and byways, some point out).

Since the semi-autonomous cars require a human driver, such cars aren't particularly important to the boomerang kids matter. There is essentially no difference between using a Level 2 or Level 3 versus a conventional car when it comes to the boomerang kids' aspects.

It is notable to point out that in spite of those dopes that keep posting videos of themselves falling asleep at the wheel of a Level 2 or Level 3 car, do not be misled into believing that you can take away your attention from the driving task while driving a semi-autonomous car.

You are the responsible party for the driving actions of the car, regardless of how much automation might be tossed into a Level 2 or Level 3.

Positive Impacts Of Self-Driving Cars

One of the predicted aspects of self-driving cars is that they will radically increase access to ridesharing. Presumably, self-driving cars will be almost non-stop, roving and roaming, awaiting a request to get you from point A to point B.

This could potentially make transit less arduous and more friction-free.

Suppose your boomerang kid comes home to live and the only jobs nearby are low paying. He or she would like to live at home for a brief period to save up money, but the closest jobs won't suffice for banking away enough dough to get out on their own anytime soon.

Via the advent of true self-driving cars, the boomerang kid might be able to take a better job further away, let's assume a higher paying position, and use the driverless car to get them to and from work.

The parent doesn't have to drive their offspring to work. The workplace can be further away from home. The young adult can catch some rest while undertaking the commute since they don't need to drive the car and instead the AI is doing the driving.

Win-win.

Another avenue for some of the boomerang kids as an initial job could fit into some of the new kinds of jobs that I have predicted will emerge to coincide with the advent of self-driving cars.

For example, there will be a new position of being a self-driving car chaperone or nanny, if you will. This role consists of riding in a driverless car to assist others that want to make use of a driverless car.

Currently, if you arrange for an Uber or Lyft, the odds are that the human driver might be willing to help someone get into the car or get out of the car. With self-driving cars, there is no human driver and therefore no one can offer a helping hand.

There is also going to be the issue of having children ride around in self-driving cars and doing so without any adult supervision in the driverless car. When you send your kids off to school in a self-driving car, and though you as an adult don't need to go along, what happens if the kids get suddenly sick while inside the car or have some emergency occur?

My guess is that we'll see essentially chaperones or nannies on wheels.

As part of the cost of using a self-driving car, you'll be able to specify whether the driverless car should have someone inside that can provide adult supervision, presumably an appropriately vetted and responsible ride-along.

Given the anticipated volume of driverless car use, the odds are that we'll need lots of these new workers.

For a boomerang kid, it would be an easy starter job and get them practiced in social interaction, building or enhancing their customer service skills.

This kind of position can also be expanded to include running errands for people.

In our gig economy, we've seen an expansion of online services that allow you to book someone to take care of your daily errands. With the click of a keyboard, you can request someone to get your clothes at the cleaners or take your dog for a walk.

Boomerang kids could become independent contractors that perform errands, doing so in conjunction with the use of self-driving cars.

Again, these aren't necessarily aspirational roles, but at least it gets the boomerang kids into the real-world, making some money and gaining work experience.

In fact, many companies won't hire a recent college grad until they have gotten some work experience under their belt, which is ironic since those post-college youths often can't get anyone to hire them for their first job. It's a frustrating Catch-22.

Via the predicted appearance of self-driving car-related jobs, the boomerang kids can start to rack-up real-world experience.

Boosting Boomerangs More So

Pundits tend to believe that self-driving cars will be owned solely by large companies that assemble large fleets of driverless cars.

According to that theory, individual ownership of cars will fall by the wayside and nobody other than big firms will own driverless cars.

I'm a bit of a contrarian in that I believe there will still be individual ownership of cars, and yes that includes true self-driving cars.

My assertion is that there will be an entire cottage industry of individual ownership of self-driving cars.

Despite the belief that driverless cars will be extremely costly, you'd be willing to get a sizable loan or fork over a chunk of your savings if you knew that the driverless car would make money for you. Today, we buy cars and don't expect them to be moneymakers. In the future, we'll expect and assume that's what cars are for.

Enterprising individuals and families will buy a driverless car for their own use and make money. After using the driverless car to get to work for the day, the rest of the time it will be available on a network for use by paying ridesharing passengers. The same goes for nighttime when the owner is asleep at home.

Here's where the boomerang kids help connect the dots.

You might decide that a good "first job" for your offspring would be to manage the activities of your driverless car.

I say this because there will be an administrative effort required to track how the self-driving car is doing in terms of making money. Someone too will need to make sure that the proper maintenance is being undertaken, and that repairs take place on a timely basis.

Each moment that the driverless car is not in a ready mode for ridesharing is lost revenue.

A boomerang kid could be tasked with doing the accounting of your small business that owns and oversees the money-making self-driving car. They would also coordinate the driverless car use and ensure that the maintenance and repairs are being done as needed.

This would be a great experience at being an entrepreneur and open their eyes to the elements that go into running a business.

Indeed, I could imagine that some exceptionally resourceful boomerang kids will perform these functions and save up to buy their own driverless car, expanding upon the family enterprise of using self-driving cars as a side income.

Conclusion

Overall, the use of self-driving cars has the potential of reducing the amount of time that a boomerang kid might end-up residing at home.

Those boomerang kids can leverage driverless cars to choose jobs that might be higher paying and further away from home, allowing them to save money faster, and therefore sooner be able to live on their own.

The responsibility involved in overseeing a family-owned driverless car could provide initial job experience and spur the boomerang kids toward entrepreneurial efforts.

Plus, once a boomerang kid moves out, they can potentially live in a safer and less expensive apartment by living say in the suburbs and commuting to work in the crowded downtown city area, using a driverless car to readily make the commute tolerable.

There's both a push and a pull effect that self-driving cars can have on the boomerang kids' phenomenon.

Unfortunately, we don't yet know when self-driving cars will become widespread, and nor do we know what the cost of ridesharing with a driverless car will be. It could be that we are years away from being able to immerse driverless cars into the boomerang kid equation.

The aim to bounce out boomerang kids is partially sought to reduce the drain on parents, some of whom might allow their entire retirement savings to be consumed by allowing their offspring to remain at home. That's not good for the parents and the inadvertent woes that they might suffer down-the-road when they are nearly penniless upon reaching retirement age.

My view is that most boomerang kids find themselves in a pickle and they are searching for a viable means to extricate themselves from it. They don't particularly want to stay at home, and they are unsure of the drain on their parents, who might be hiding it from the offspring to bravely show their unhesitating support and love for their kids.

Self-driving cars could be an innovation that aids the boomerang kids and simultaneously aids the parents. It could be a tool that will spur a faster and better bounce, keeping the boomerang from conking anybody on the head and knocking them out of life's pursuits.

CHAPTER 9
WAYMO COMING TO L.A.
AND
AI SELF-DRIVING CARS

CHAPTER 9

WAYMO COMING TO L.A.
AND AI SELF-DRIVING CARS

Hey, fellow Los Angelans, get ready, Waymo is bringing its vaunted self-driving cars to Los Angeles.

Time to roll out the red carpet for the esteemed arrival.

To clarify, there is the city of Los Angeles (population of about 4 million), which is a subset of the larger county of Los Angeles (total population of about 10 million, encompassing over 100 cities), of which most people think of "Los Angeles" as the entire county, complete with the celebrity-laden Hollywood area, the sandy and wave-crushing surfing beaches, the bustling downtown L.A. area with its ever-rising skyscrapers, and enough other varied habitats to declare this place as a bubbling and intertwining series of city-varying biomes.

Maybe you've heard of Arcadia, Artesia, Beverly Hills, Burbank, Carson, Cerritos, Culver City, El Segundo, Glendale, Hermosa Beach, Inglewood, Irwindale, La Mirada, Long Beach, Malibu, Manhattan Beach, Paramount, Pasadena, Redondo Beach, San Gabriel, Santa Monica, West Hollywood, amid the slew of local cities in L.A. county.

All told, L.A. county comes to nearly 4,800 square miles.

For anyone seeking to put a self-driving car through its paces, coming to L.A. puts you into one of the biggest and potentially baddest places to see what your driverless car can do.

There are already about 8 million cars registered in the county of Los Angeles, and it seems that nearly all of them want to drive around at the same time, being joined too by hundreds of thousands of cars being used to commute into the county area each day from other surrounding cities of Southern California.

One estimate is that the cars roaming and puttering within Los Angeles drive a staggering 222 million miles, per day (yes, that's each day), which is both a source of pride and a sorrowful matter.

The sorrow comes from the massive traffic snarls and the sluggish drive times to get across town, along with the voluminous fender benders and car crashes (in L.A. City, there are over 50,000 car accidents per year, and that's just in that one city).

A distance of 20 miles, a rather common distance traversed to get from one part of town to the other, which in theory could be driven at a speed of 60 miles per hour via open freeway speeds in a mere twenty minutes time is much more likely to take an hour, or perhaps an hour and a half to even two hours, depending upon the time of day and the luck of the draw.

Forget about the concept of open freeways and your hair cheerfully wafting in the wind as you zip along in your speedster. Those days are long past.

We also reportedly have some of the worst roads in the entire United States.

Stats show that car owners here need to spend an average of about $921 extra per year on automobile repairs, maintenance efforts, and added fuel consumption to contend with our lousy roads.

Potholes, yep, we've got them, lots of them.

Cracked asphalt and streets that look as though heavy military tank treads have driven over them, sure, they are aplenty.

Faded street surface markers and confounding painted lines on the roadways, allegedly there to provide driving guidance, those are here too.

It's a bonanza for any self-driving car maker that wishes to have their vehicles travel over the adventurous and arduous 22,000 miles of public roadways, or maybe it's more of a potential headache and heartache that will prove to be a trying experience for driverless cars.

One could argue that if a self-driving car can make it here, it can make it anywhere (humble apologizes to New York City which thinks of itself in those terms).

Waymo's First Actions Here

Currently, Waymo has started undertaking an extensive mapping activity of having a few of their specially outfitted data-collecting vehicles crisscross the Los Angeles area.

These vehicles contain a state-of-the-art barrage of sensory equipment, the idea is to first map out the area and then use those maps to get the self-driving cars ready for hitting our streets.

You might be puzzled that such mapping is being undertaken since certainly one would assume that Google has already mapped the Los Angeles region, which it has.

The conventional mapping did not go as in-depth as does this specially performed new mapping. Tons of added data of a 3D nature and including subtle but significant aspects like where the curbs are, and the locations of intersection traffic signals are considered a savvy aspect to have in-hand for their driverless car efforts.

It is widely known that Waymo's self-driving cars have been cruising around the Silicon Valley area (that's Northern California, not Southern California), and notably undertaking a pronounced tryout effort in the Phoenix area, doing so with a human back-up driver in their vehicles as a safety precaution.

Many would assume that coming to another locale, such as Los Angeles, should be a piece of cake.

Toss in some maps of the local area, and voila, you've got your self-driving car primed to rove here and there in Los Angeles.

Well, one could try doing it that way, but the odds are that any such ill-prepared self-driving car is going to experience a lot of difficulties and unknowns.

Readying a self-driving car for a new locale like Los Angeles, encompassing a confounding variety of roadway infrastructure, plus the cultural norms of how drivers drive here, plus the antics of pedestrians and bicyclists in the L.A. region, and other nuances are likely different than what has been encountered in other places.

In that sense, after potentially conquering driving in Los Angeles (assuming they can), the ability to replant their self-driving cars in many other areas of the United States will have a much stronger leg-up, having dealt with the diversity of driving challenges here.

I realize we don't have the kind of adverse weather that one would experience in the Midwest or East coast, and thus the odds of having the AI learn about snow-related driving or dealing with sheets of ice on the roads is relatively slim. Nonetheless, you gain a lot of hefty and valued driving experience by figuring out how to drive in Southern California.

Besides, we're also known for a rather snarky trick, you can go to the beach in the morning and catch the waves, and then head-up to the local mountains in a two-hour drive and be in the snow, going skiing and making snowmen. Thus, in one day, you can readily experience both sunshine and dry roads, coupled with snowfall and icy roadway conditions.

One supposes that a self-driving car could do the same trick if you wanted it to get experience in both warm weather and cold weather. As a helpful suggestion, the human back-up drivers should probably bring their skis and heavy jacket in the driverless car, being ready to make such a journey at a moment's notice, if the snowfall conditions warrant such a quick trip (okay, I'm half-joking about this).

Levels Of Self-Driving Cars

It is important to clarify what I mean when referring to self-driving cars, which has become a misused and confusing phrase.

True self-driving cars are ones that the AI drives the car entirely on its own and there isn't any human assistance during the driving task.

These driverless cars are considered a Level 4 and Level 5, while a car that requires a human driver to co-share the driving effort is usually considered at a Level 2 or Level 3. The cars that co-share the driving task are described as being semi-autonomous, and typically contain a variety of automated add-ons that are referred to as ADAS (Advanced Driver-Assistance Systems).

There is not yet a true self-driving car at Level 5, which we don't yet even know if this will be possible to achieve, and nor how long it will take to get there.

Meanwhile, the Level 4 efforts are gradually trying to get some traction by undergoing very narrow and selective public roadway trials, though there is controversy over whether this testing should be allowed per se (we are all life-or-death guinea pigs in an experiment taking place on our highways and byways, some point out).

It is notable to point out that in spite of those dimwits that keep posting videos of themselves falling asleep at the wheel of a Level 2 or Level 3 car, do not be misled into believing that you can take away your attention from the driving task while driving a semi-autonomous car.

You are the responsible party for the driving actions of the car, regardless of how much automation might be tossed into a Level 2 or Level 3.

The general public oftentimes does not realize what Waymo is trying to do in comparison to many of the other companies striving toward arriving at truly self-driving cars.

There are essentially two major kinds of strategies involved in seeking true self-driving cars.

One strategy involves focusing on Level 2 and Level 3 cars, and then incrementally trying to turn those into Level 4 and Level 5 cars. This is a stepwise refinement approach.

Another strategy, the one being employed by Waymo, involves leaping over the Level 2 and Level 3, allowing them to concentrate entirely and solely on achieving Level 4 and Level 5.

As I've exhorted many times, the dangers for those immersed in the Level 2 and Level 3 is that you are including humans in co-sharing the driving task, and for which there are a lot of chances of things going awry. Some assert that Level 3 cars are going to be a quagmire of co-shared car crashes and incidents.

Fingers will be pointed at the human driver and fingers will be pointed at the semi-autonomous automation. It's going to be a mess.

Partially to avoid that kind of lawsuit laden bog, Waymo is instead aiming to get to the moonshot of a true self-driving car by bypassing the intermediary levels.

They have been doggedly pursuing this strategy for many years.

Keep in mind that it is tempting to ratchet downward into the Level 2 and Level 3, allowing one to almost immediately monetize and commercialize your driving automation. Meanwhile, trying to get much dough out of Level 4 self-driving cars is going to be limited, until and if the Level 4 capabilities can be advanced sufficiently to run on their own without a human back-up driver, and safely so.

Google has had deep enough pockets to take a gamble on swinging for the fence, while many of the traditional automakers weren't able or willing to make the same bet.

The head of an automaker has to serve two masters, their need to put new cars into the marketplace today and thus earn money in doing so, while also keeping an eye towards the future and not get caught holding the bag if others achieve true self-driving cars and they did not.

As I've mentioned previously, this explains why there are so many partnerships and coopetition arrangements occurring in the self-driving car realm. Everyone realizes the steep risks involved in trying to arrive at true self-driving cars and are seeking ways to spread the risk and the costs involved in getting there.

Community Awareness

There's a famous model of change that was promulgated by Kurt Lewin and postulates that anytime you introduce change you should be undertaking three steps, namely preparing for the change, performing of the change, and then solidifying the change.

I bring this up because the act of introducing self-driving cars into a locale needs to be done via making use of those three steps.

A self-driving car is a form of innovation and must be treated as a change or disrupter to today's transportation modes.

Unfortunately, some of the earlier efforts to bring self-driving cars into a new location were done in a typically tech affronting manner. Suddenly, driverless cars were seen around a town, and nobody knew what they were doing there.

One of my favorite stories is the one about a cop that stopped a self-driving vehicle and was concerned about the fact that it appeared to be void of a driver. That's not a good way to make yourself part of the neighborhood.

Surveys already show that the American public is skeptical of driverless cars, including that around three-fourths are concerned or fearful about the advent of self-driving cars.

If you abruptly parachute self-driving cars into a city or town, the odds are that rather than being welcomed with open arms, you might have some coming after you with pitchforks and rightfully worried that Frankenstein has arrived.

Fortunately, the self-driving car companies have learned the lesson of being more neighborly and are gradually doing a better job of introducing themselves into each new locale.

In that manner, the act of Waymo starting their mapping efforts is akin to the first step of the Lewin model, essentially getting Los Angeles ready for the arrival of Waymo's self-driving cars. The mapping process is quite benign, and yet it effectively says in bold letters that change is coming.

Ease your way into the market, that's an astute way to proceed.

One can speculate about ways to further gain traction in the Los Angeles region.

When the timing is right, perhaps invite some celebrities to take a ride in a Waymo self-driving car, which would catch the eye of the media here and globally. It would also get the gossipy side of town to spread the word, which maybe is even stronger than everyday media proclamations.

We've also got our lauded Vision Zero initiative that has had a lot of fanfare by Los Angeles politicians and other local officials. I've been saying all along that self-driving cars could be a mighty contributor to the Vision Zero goals.

Critics of the Vision Zero effort are quick to point out that despite the program being launched some three years ago, hoping to eliminate traffic deaths by the year 2025, hundreds of such deaths are still taking place each year.

There are lots of ways that Waymo might decide to wine and dine Los Angeles as part of the collegial bonding of having self-driving cars roam around the region.

Another idea would be to consider connecting with some of the local universities, such as USC and UCLA, allowing for college students to be some of the first participants in a driverless car passenger program akin to the one taking place in Phoenix.

Gaining the hearts and minds of millennials, and boosting their interests in STEM (science, technology, engineering, and math) would seem like a handy means of achieving multiple birds with one stone.

Conclusion

It won't be all roses and bright sunshine here in Los Angeles for the introduction of driverless cars.

As a dual-edged sword, the kind of publicity that can be achieved by using self-driving cars here is astronomical and could be a huge boon, though if an incident occurs, the same level of heightened attention could cause the megaphone to turn on a dime and loudly denounce driverless cars.

We can be hot or cold here, whichever way the wind is blowing that day (more so than just the Santa Ana winds).

You can anticipate that Los Angeles pedestrians will want to exercise their curiosity and innate cynicism, trying to prank any self-driving cars that they see (for more about the pranking of driverless cars, see my piece here).

Imagine too a bunch of self-driving cars that get mired in bumper-to-bumper L.A. traffic, suffering the same indignity that the rest of us daily endure. Sad, but true.

Local drivers often do Sudoku puzzles or try to learn a foreign language while stuck at the wheel of their car.

Maybe self-driving cars can turn their pumped-up computer processors, working rather idly while in no-go go-slow situations, toward calculating pi to the longest number of digits or participate in the SETI program to detect whether there are aliens on other planets beaming radio waves at us (there are a lot of Los Angeles residents that already think they are receiving such signals directly to their noggins).

Shouldn't driverless cars be a forerunner of reducing traffic, and yet they will at first regrettably contribute to traffic.

Though you could certainly argue that the number of self-driving cars will be a drop in the bucket in comparison to the millions of everyday cars on the roads, a picture could be worth a thousand words and people will simply be disgruntled to see that there are more cars, albeit even self-driving cars, adding to the traffic snarls.

Heisenberg's uncertainty principle also comes to play here.

Essentially, his principle is that the act of measuring something will often tend to impact the very thing you are measuring.

In the case of self-driving cars, human drivers in cars nearby a self-driving car are bound to change their driving behavior due to realizing they are next to a self-driving car.

Initially, these human drivers will perhaps give a wider berth to the self-driving car, which likely means a worsening of traffic, and lamentably does less good for the Machine Learning aspects of a driverless car due to the artificially created gentleness fostered in local driving behaviors.

Los Angeles drivers though are pretty much used to all kinds of spectacles on our roadways, including dropped couches, ladders, standalone toilets oddly sitting on the roadway, wandering animals such as a family of ducks and a small herd of cattle, etc.

We become immune to seeing something that surprises us.

Once the self-driving cars have been doting around for a while, the odds are that these roving wonderments will get the same treatment as any other car on the roadway. This means those driverless cars will get summarily cut off in traffic, treated like an enemy of the roadway, since we tend to believe that all other drivers are dolts (human or otherwise) and nearby cars are merely irritants standing in our own way to get expeditiously to where we want to go.

Dudes and dudettes, give Waymo a chance, and as a tip for Waymo, it's up to you to become a bona fide Angeleno, taking Los Angeles not by storm but instead as a welcome relief to a future whereby we might have less snarled traffic, fewer adverse car-related incidents, and be riding around as La La Land passengers, singing and cherishing our fine weather here in true self-driving cars.

I'll surf to that future.

CHAPTER 10

GETTING TO SCALE

AND

AI SELF-DRIVING CARS

CHAPTER 10

GETTING TO SCALE

AND

AI SELF-DRIVING CARS

Scaling up your business, getting to scale, wanting to reach scale, these are all part of today's buzzwords about "scale" that businesses and investors are repeatedly exhorting.

Like many such oft said words, after a while the overuse of the word scale seems to gradually get diluted or used as nothing more than a self-serving grandiose punchline.

Numerous founders and business executives' resort to claiming that they are aiming to get to scale, yet there's frequently little substantive evidence to explain how or when scale will be reached.

What does it mean to seek or reach a scale?

Generally, for start-ups, the notion is that you sometimes start relatively small, perhaps making a prototype or a minimally viable product (MVP), and show it off to gain attention and funding. Potential investors and actual investors are usually of the belief that the one-time version of your product can become a mass-produced one.

This is not always the case or might be exorbitantly costly to achieve.

Something that you might have hand-crafted could be terribly difficult and expensive to recreate and produce on any sizable volume.

Furthermore, your product might work for a handful of situations that you tested, but once it is put into wider use, you could unexpectedly discover that it has limitations or flaws of a fatal kind or that constrain your market potential for the product.

Here's then the question for the day: Will self-driving cars be able to scale?

Many outside the driverless car industry are assuming that if you can make one self-driving car, you can make zillions of them. This assumption is not necessarily the case.

Let's unpack the matter.

Clarifying The Levels Of Self-Driving Cars

It is important to clarify what I mean when referring to true self-driving cars.

True self-driving cars are ones that the AI drives the car entirely on its own and there isn't any human assistance during the driving task.

These driverless cars are considered a Level 4 and Level 5, while a car that requires a human driver to co-share the driving effort is usually considered at a Level 2 or Level 3. The cars that co-share the driving task are described as being semi-autonomous, and typically contain a variety of automated add-ons that are referred to as ADAS (Advanced Driver-Assistance Systems).

There is not yet a true self-driving car at Level 5, which we don't yet even know if this will be possible to achieve, and nor how long it will take to get there.

Meanwhile, the Level 4 efforts are gradually trying to get some traction by undergoing very narrow and selective public roadway trials, though there is controversy over whether this testing should be allowed per se (we are all life-or-death guinea pigs in an experiment taking place on our highways and byways, some point out).

Since the semi-autonomous cars require a human driver, such cars aren't particularly important to the scaling question. There is essentially no difference between using a Level 2 or Level 3 versus a conventional car when it comes to a matter of scale.

It is notable to point out that in spite of those dopes that keep posting videos of themselves falling asleep at the wheel of a Level 2 or Level 3 car, do not be misled into believing that you can take away your attention from the driving task while driving a semi-autonomous car.

You are the responsible party for the driving actions of the car, regardless of how much automation might be tossed into a Level 2 or Level 3.

Scaling Of Autonomous Cars

True self-driving cars are chock full of specialized sensors, including cameras, radar, LIDAR, ultrasonic units, and various other advanced electronics.

Currently, the driverless cars that are being tried out on our roadways are few and far between, especially when you consider that the number of conventional cars in the United States alone is about 250 million.

The number of (somewhat) self-driving cars is a tiny drop in the bucket of the total car population.

Pundits that believe in a magical future are prone to suggesting that someday soon we'll have all self-driving cars and no remaining conventional cars. The hope is that by getting rid of all conventional cars, including Level 2 and Level 3 semi-autonomous cars, there won't be any pesky and car crashing human drivers anymore.

Well, let's be serious and agree that there's no economically sound way that we would all overnight discard our conventional cars and instead adopt true self-driving cars.

By magic wand, even if we all did agree to stop using our conventional cars, consider the length of time it would take to ramp-up and produce enough self-driving cars to handle the needed volume of driving in the U.S. alone (approximately 3.12 trillion miles per year).

The scaling aspect is a serious one and not just because of the automobile manufacturing efforts.

Many of the specialized sensors that are being used in today's experimental self-driving cars are not being sold in the millions upon millions of numbers of units. Thus, those sensor makers would need to scale-up to produce enough of their sensors to fit onto the millions upon millions of self-driving cars that we'll presumably be seeing built and fielded.

As an aside, the upside potential of riding the self-driving car gravy train is part of the reason that many of the sensor makers are fighting fiercely to get into the experiments taking place today for self-driving cars. Their hope is that by becoming the default sensor for a particular driverless car, their product will surf the massive wave ahead as millions upon millions of self-driving cars are ultimately made and sold.

One important aspect to keep in mind is that the existing experimental tryouts of self-driving cars are being undertaken in a very controlled and small-sized manner.

Once self-driving cars are available in the wild, presumably, the driverless cars will be used as much as possible, running maybe 24 x 7 if possible. This makes sense to get your monies worth out of the self-driving car. Plus, if demand is going to shoot through the roof for ridership, the odds are that the driverless cars will be in-motion much or most of the time.

Can the sensors being used today on driverless car tryouts handle the rigors of the real world on an ongoing and extensive basis?

We don't really know if the sensors can handle reality and the hardships of being used all of the time.

Pretty much most of the existing driverless car tryouts are being overseen by topnotch maintenance crews. These master crews make sure that the moment a sensor even burps, it gets replaced. Also, when the driverless car comes into the special facility for an evening's rest, the sensors and other parts of the self-driving car are reviewed to make sure all is in tiptop shape.

It is doubtful that any massive rollout of self-driving cars could entertain the same kind of handholding.

On a scaling factor, we don't know if the sensors can scale-up to high usage and the real-world environment of harsh weather, people that bang their shopping carts into your parked driverless car, and the other daily abuses that our everyday cars deal with.

Human Scaling Aspects

Another scaling factor involves people.

There are some automakers that insist that their self-driving cars will only need to ask a human rider their desired destination, and otherwise, no further interaction is needed.

That's nutty.

Humans riding in today's Uber and Lyft cars that are driven by a human driver are known for asking and directing the drivers in zillions of varying ways. The need for an actual conversation is important in many ridesharing circumstances.

Can the limited Natural Language Processing (NLP) that an Alexa or Siri provides today be scaled to handle the fluent driving-related conversations that human riders will demand?

Researchers are toiling away at this, but the fluent AI-driver does not yet exist.

Also, what happens when a passenger suddenly starts choking on that leftover T-bone steak that they brought into the self-driving car as a late-night snack?

By removing a human driver from the driverless car, you are removing too the human actions that a driver might render beyond the sole act of driving a car.

Will the notion of not having a human driver be able to scale in the sense that passengers will no longer have a fellow human in the car with them?

AI Scaling Aspects

Most of the current tryouts of driverless cars are taking place in confined geographical areas, such as in a restricted area of Phoenix, Las Vegas, San Francisco, and the like.

Will an AI self-driving car readily scale-up to be a good driver in other places?

Some believe that driverless cars can only work properly if the chosen geographic area has been exhaustively mapped and remapped. If that's the case, the effort and cost to do that mapping might preclude being able to easily have the self-driving car drive in other parts of the country.

Via the use of Machine Learning and Deep Learning, the AI is supposed to get better and better at driving.

Of course, if the self-driving car is only driving in the same place over-and-over, the odds are that it isn't learning new things about driving that might well be encountered in other locations. This is like a teenage novice driver that gets used to driving in their own neighborhood and then is terrified to drive on open highways or places they've never driven on.

One criticism of the U.S. based driverless car efforts has been that the focus on driving in the United States is leading to self-driving cars that are only familiar with U.S. driving aspects, including the legal requirements and the cultural rules-of-the-road elements.

Will the AI systems be scalable to drive in international settings?

Some believe it will be a child's play and merely the changing of a few parameters in the software, but anyone that has driven in countries around the world knows that it is harder to switch and adjust to foreign driving practices than it might seem on the surface.

Volume Scaling

An often-quoted estimate provided by Intel suggests that each driverless car will generate at least 4GB of data per day (likely more), based upon all the camera images and video collected, the radar data collected, and so on.

In theory, the data is going to be pushed up to the cloud of the automaker or tech firm that made the AI systems for the self-driving car, a process known as OTA (Over-The-Air) updating.

On a scaling basis, this means a ton of electronic communications across networks, along with a ton of storage that will be needed in the cloud. Multiply 4GB by 250 million cars by 365 days of the year, and the volume is daunting.

Self-driving cars are going to be communicating with each other via V2V (vehicle-to-vehicle) electronic communication. This will be handy since a self-driving car that encounters a cow in the roadway can electronically alert any upcoming driverless cars that are nearing that juncture of a highway.

Today, the use of V2V among self-driving cars is sparse or non-existent.

On a scaling basis, what happens once thousands of self-driving cars are zooming along on a freeway and they are all sending out a bombardment of V2V messages to each other?

Conclusion

Automakers and tech firms are focused on making baby steps right now. Their aim is to produce a self-driving car that can safely drive on our roadways.

Worrying about scale is not quite as crucial, especially if you aren't even sure that you can get a self-driving car to function at an autonomous level.

This is often the stance of inventors that are making something brand new that has never existed before. They are concerned primarily with getting the darned invention itself to work. They assume or hope that scaling will eventually be possible, though it's not necessarily at top-of-mind and a matter that they figure can be deferred until it, later on, becomes paramount.

You might be familiar with the famous story about Thomas Edison and the invention of the light bulb, though you've likely only heard the version that's a half-truth.

Edison and his crew tested around 6,000 different materials as the filament for a light bulb.

Light bulbs already existed, but they were generally impractical due to the filament being overly costly and so flimsy that it wouldn't last very long.

After thousands of trials using different kinds of filaments, he finally found one that was the Goldilocks version, strong enough to last sufficiently and inexpensive enough to be real-world practical.

I tell the story because Edison's efforts weren't per se about inventing the light bulb and instead dealt with making a light bulb that could be scalable.

For self-driving cars, we are still in the period prior to having a working light bulb, as it were, and once we do have a working one the race will be on to figure out how it can be scaled-up.

Scale will matter since having self-driving cars that can only work in narrow ways in narrow places will not be much of a money maker and perhaps be discounted as toy-like efforts rather than something applicable to the real-world.

Scaling up could be the fly in the ointment of self-driving car emergence.

CHAPTER 11

LOOKING ALIKE

AND

AI SELF-DRIVING CARS

CHAPTER 11

LOOKING ALIKE

AND

AI SELF-DRIVING CARS

Have you ever seen a sea of yellow cabs, all of which seem indistinguishable from each other?

It used to be that if you booked a yellow cab for picking you up at a busy airport or similar venue, the odds were that a slew of other yellow cabs were also vying for picking up passengers there too. As such, you would have a tough time trying to figure out which among the multitudes of yellow cabs was the one designated just for you.

The cabs sometimes had a number displayed on the outside of the vehicle, and in theory, you could then spot your particular yellow cab, but possessing the number was one tricky aspect and the other was the arduous difficulty of trying to clearly see the number among the blur of so many cabs.

There was pretty much little point in reserving a cab beforehand and instead, it seemed wiser to take a chance at randomly hailing a cab.

Today's world is a sea change, as it were.

When you wait for today's Uber or Lyft ridesharing pick-ups, you are informed via your mobile app that the car is a specific make, model, and color, along with getting a heads-up about the driver of the vehicle. Plus, since the drivers are all driving their own cars, there is inherently a diversity in the make, models, and colors of the cars.

It's usually relatively easy to spy the reserved ridesharing car that is intending to be your ride.

Here's a bit of a twist in the future.

The expectation is that by-and-large self-driving cars will all look alike, at least with respect to a specific make, model, and possibly even color.

When you hail a self-driving car to come pick you up and assuming that you are at a crowded venue like a baseball game or an airport, the odds are that hundreds or maybe thousands of similar-looking driverless cars will all be vying to pick-up passengers at the same time and in the same place.

In a sense, it will be a rebirth of the indistinguishable yellow cab era.

What will true self-driving cars do or become to standout amongst the crowd and be readily identifiable by prospective riders?

Let's unpack the matter.

Defining The Levels Of Self-Driving Cars

It is important to clarify what I mean when referring to true self-driving cars.

True self-driving cars are ones that the AI drives the car entirely on its own and there isn't any human assistance during the driving task.

These driverless cars are considered a Level 4 and Level 5, while a car that requires a human driver to co-share the driving effort is usually considered at a Level 2 or Level 3. The cars that co-share the driving task are described as being semi-autonomous, and typically contain a variety of automated add-ons that are referred to as ADAS (Advanced Driver-Assistance Systems).

There is not yet a true self-driving car at Level 5, which we don't yet even know if this will be possible to achieve, and nor how long it will take to get there.

Meanwhile, the Level 4 efforts are gradually trying to get some traction by undergoing very narrow and selective public roadway trials, though there is controversy over whether this testing should be allowed per se (we are all life-or-death guinea pigs in an experiment taking place on our highways and byways, some point out).

Since the semi-autonomous cars require a human driver, such cars aren't particularly significant to the yellow cab problem per se. There is essentially no difference between using a Level 2 or Level 3 versus a conventional car when it comes to providing a ridesharing service.

It is notable to point out that in spite of those dimwits that keep posting videos of themselves falling asleep at the wheel of a Level 2 or Level 3 car, do not be misled into believing that you can take away your attention from the driving task while driving a semi-autonomous car.

You are the responsible party for the driving actions of the car, regardless of how much automation might be tossed into a Level 2 or Level 3.

Self-Driving Cars That Look-Alike

For Level 4 and Level 5 self-driving cars, the automakers and tech firms are currently focusing on having one specific kind of make, model, and color for their respective experimental efforts.

Thus, automaker X might have chosen a certain make, model, and color for their driverless car foray, meaning that right now all their eggs are in that particular basket.

This makes sense due to wanting to have a stable platform for testing out the self-driving tech aspects.

It wouldn't be prudent to try doing so with a variety of differing car models since the automaker might not know whether the automobile itself is creating an issue, rather than the cause being the driverless tech components.

The rule-of-thumb is to pick one relatively stable and known car as a base platform and get the self-driving stack to play well on that automobile. In theory, the driverless stuff will be somewhat portable over to other makes and models, though that's not a guaranteed slam dunk and don't be holding your breath that just because something works well on car A it will also work readily on car B.

The color chosen for the driverless cars being used on our roadways today is often established to showcase the brand of the automaker or tech firm that's doing the trials. Thus, automaker Y might decide to paint all their self-driving cars as blue and white, along with having their company logo proudly displayed on the hood of the vehicle.

One open question will be whether the automakers will want or need to vary the painted colors on their self-driving cars.

Some believe that in the early days of the advent of driverless cars, the automakers and tech firms are going to want to purposely ensure that everyone knows that the self-driving car cruising around our neighborhoods is their pride and joy. The odds are that the make, model, and color will be the same as what was used when first experimenting with their driverless efforts. Keep it straightforward and simple, doing so to brandish and cement your brand in the eyes of the public.

Returning to the yellow cab problem, suppose you are at a concert and opt to use your mobile phone to reserve a driverless car as a pick-up at the end of the musical event.

You come out of the concert, maybe half-drunk, but let's put that aside for the moment, and eagerly look for your reserved self-driving car.

Lo and behold, there are a hundred driverless cars of automaker Z that have arrived, each waiting to pick-up a concertgoer that opted to reserve a ride.

Which one is there for you?

It could be problematic for you to know.

That being said, let's also be clear that there might be hundreds of automaker Q's driverless cars that have also arrived, and so at least you would presumably know by immediate sight that none of those were at the concert to pick you up.

Okay, the yellow cab dilemma is resurfacing and there needs to be a fix or resolution.

Ways To Cope With The Look-Alike

Consider the various ways to cope with the look-alike problem:

• Flash The Headlights. In a quite low-tech approach, a self-driving car could flash its headlights once it gets close to the person being picked-up. Presumably, you would know that the driverless car is your ride when you see the headlights flashing. This method is handy for the automakers since there are no add-ons needed to do this, and an already available component of the car is being used. A big downside is that there might be hundreds of driverless cars all flashing their headlights at the same time, which would make them indistinguishable, plus maybe a bit scary to see (whoa, they are all flashing their headlights, run for the hills!).

• Display A Number. Like having yellow cabs display a number on the outside of the vehicle, a self-driving car could have a painted number or a static display showing a number. The ridesharing passenger would be notified of the number via their mobile app. This would work though it could be exasperating to find your specific pick-up as the sea of numbers might be close enough to your number that you'll get confused and try to get into the wrong self-driving car. User error.

• Use An External LED. Another approach would be to mount an LED display on the rooftop of the driverless car and have it display a number or maybe the name of the person being picked-up. This would be easier to have your spot, but it also adds more cost to an already expensive self-driving car. Also, it would be crucial to ensure that the LED device does not disturb or disrupt any of the driving sensors that might also be mounted on the rooftop. By the way, even if automakers don't provide an external LED, you can bet that some enterprising entrepreneurs will rush to market with such displays.

- Toot The Horn. Like the idea of flashing headlights, the AI system could toot the horn to alert awaiting rider. Maybe two toots, a pause, and two more toots might be your signal. The problem with this solution is that if there are hundreds of driverless cars coming up to do pick-ups, the cacophony of blaring horns could be overpowering. Put this option into the repugnant category since we already have too much noise pollution on our streets.

- Communicate Via V2X. Driverless cars are going to be outfitted with electronic communications capabilities, generally known as V2X (vehicle-to-everything). The self-driving car could send out a message to your smartphone and let you know where the driverless car is. This is bound to help find your specific ride, though it has some downsides to it too, including that your smartphone must have a solid signal for you to receive the messages emanating from the driverless car.

- Phone Call With The Driverless Car. Another approach involves having the AI system talk with the ridesharing passenger by making a phone call and using its Natural Language Processing (NLP) feature. In an Alexa or Siri kind of mode, the self-driving car could call you, and interact with you as it gets close to your location. One supposes it could do other things at the same time such as tell you about the prevailing weather and maybe brighten your waiting time by telling a joke or two.

- Audio Emission. Self-driving cars might end-up being outfitted with external speakers to allow for the AI to converse with nearby pedestrians. As your driverless car pick-up arrives, it might start shouting out your name, such as saying hey, Lauren, I'm here, right over here. Once again, this is not going to be effective in the setting of hundreds of self-driving cars. I'd say too that it would be eerie to hear all those driverless cars calling out people's names.

- Leverage GPS. If you have your smartphone on you while waiting for a driverless car, the AI could use your GPS calculated position to try and come as close to you as feasible. Likewise, the GPS of your smartphone would show where the self-driving car is positioned. This is akin to two strangers meeting in the night, albeit guided by electronics that detect where each of them is.

- Vary The Painted Colors. Some are quick to suggest that the automaker ought to vary the painted colors of their driverless cars, thus having some that are red, some black, some orange, etc. Yes, this might help, but the luck of the draw could be that among the hundreds of self-driving cars that come to get a bunch of exiting concert goers, you'll still have plenty that are in the same fluorescent green or whatever other colors might be used.

- Use of Advanced Car Skins. There are R&D efforts to make a type of skin that would wrap around the car body and could display different colors or shapes, maybe displaying letters or images. In this case, when a driverless car arrived at a pick-up destination, it could fully display a unique looking pattern, or maybe display the face of the person that booked the ride. Besides the potential added cost, this approach is not yet ready for prime time.

- Augmented Reality (AR). Besides using augmented reality to play Pokémon games, you could use AR to find a specific self-driving car that is trying to pick you up. By invoking an AR app on your smartphone, you would hold-up the phone to point it toward a herd of seemingly indistinguishable driverless cars, and voila, the one that is coming for you would be highlighted. This could be readily done via the AI beaming a signal to your smartphone and the app then placing a bright red circle on your screen that outlines the right driverless car for you.

- Other. There are other ways in which some are tackling this problem. For example, another idea is to have a small drone that would hover over the driverless car and then fly to the person that hailed the vehicle, doing so to guide them to their specific vehicle. Most of these other approaches are rather esoteric, yet clever and have some possibility to them.

Conclusion

A combination of the approaches could be undertaken, doing a mix-and-match.

Also, the context of the pick-up situation might dictate the best choice.

If there isn't a sea of other driverless cars, the least obtrusive method would be fine since the self-driving car will standout already.

Right now, none of us are experiencing the yellow cab problem about self-driving cars, due to the lack of driverless cars on our roadways. We won't realize the irritations involved until there is a vast number of driverless cars out there.

Many of the automakers and tech firms aren't especially worried right now about being able to find your designated driverless car. First and foremost, self-driving cars must work. Getting driverless cars to safely drive around our highways and byways is the top priority, suitably so.

For AI conspiracists, my having alleged that all self-driving cars look alike is taboo, namely that once AI takes over our world, the AI will remember my comments and seek to punish me for my insulting transgression.

May the record clearly state that I am casting no aspersions toward AI and I am a friend of AI. Please write that down, for my sake.

CHAPTER 12

NOVA DOCUMENTARY

ON

AI SELF-DRIVING CARS

CHAPTER 12

NOVA DOCUMENTARY

AND

AI SELF-DRIVING CARS

If you have any inkling of interest in the status and future of self-driving cars, you have to watch a fast-moving, well-informed, and thought-provoking (yet seat-squirming) new documentary entitled "Look Who's Driving," premiering on Wednesday, October 23, 2019, at 9 p.m. on PBS and also available for streaming that evening and thereafter at the pbs.org/nova web site.

Come to think of it, even if you don't yet have an inkling of interest about self-driving cars, you ought to anyway watch this latest informative addition to the acclaimed NOVA documentary series known for astutely covering crucial topics in science, high-tech, and engineering.

I urge you to take in this breezy 28-minute non-stop roller coaster ride that depicts the emergence of driverless cars because, whether you realize it or not, we are all currently part of a grand experiment seeking to achieve true self-driving cars.

Yes, you are already in The Matrix, as it were, but probably didn't know it.

Whether you are a human driver at the wheel and driving near to a self-driving car being trained on our public roadways, or perhaps driving a modern-day semi-autonomous car that has advanced driving tech, or even if you are merely an impatient pedestrian that dares to dodge cars while crossing the street, you have a stake in what's taking place.

Your stake entails life or death consequences.

Many are in the dark about how society is partaking in this moonshot-like endeavor that aims to get our cars to become better and better at driving. The great unwashed need to have their eyes opened and their minds put to the test about how such driverless cars are and should be advanced and fielded.

Fortunately, Look Who's Driving offers a carefully reasoned and properly balanced examination of where we are with self-driving cars and posits intelligently about where we might be heading.

Balance Is Key

Balance on this topic is often hard to find.

There are documentaries that over-inflate what today's so-called self-driving cars can do, creating unwanted confusion and lulling some into believing that their cars can drive for them, when in fact their tech-boosted car isn't yet at that level of proficiency.

Those ill-informed drivers that take a nap while at the wheel of a semi-autonomous car are putting their own life in jeopardy and the lives of those in cars nearby, plus they are endangering unsuspecting pedestrians that by a stroke of bad luck might encounter these (essentially) unguided missiles coming down their street.

On the other side of the documentary coin are the films that promote fear-mongering and end-of-the-world proselytizing that singularly pound away at the modern-day failings of self-driving cars.

Any of the one-sided takes on the matter don't seem to be willing to acknowledge and nor point out that there are calculated risks involved in how society has accepted the benefits and simultaneous pitfalls of having cars on our roads.

Put bluntly, cars and human driving today incur harsh costs associated with having these multi-ton machines that we routinely use to get around town for everyday transit. In the U.S. alone, there are about 40,000 car-related deaths each year, and an estimated 1.2 million annual deaths worldwide.

We are paying a hefty price for the use of conventional cars.

In Look Who's Driving, it was especially refreshing to see a professionally produced documentary that acknowledges the overall value proposition that inextricably pervades human driving and cars, along with confronting the issue of how the existing path toward making self-driving cars is potholed with both promise and peril.

I was invited to watch a special preview of the documentary, doing so on Friday, October 18, 2019, at the illustrious Computer History Museum (CHM) that resides in the heart of Silicon Valley.

Coupled with the screening was a panel of self-driving car luminaries that provided the assembled Friday night crowd with a lively and interactive take on what's happening now and what might happen next in the driverless car realm.

In speaking with the CEO of the Computer History Museum, tech industry superstar Dan'l Lewin, he emphasized a new vision of how the vaunted Museum is finding ways to recharge and serve as an irresistible magnetic attractor for showcasing ways that high-tech is ever-changing and impacting all our lives.

Having come on-board to the CHM about a year ago, Dan'l is primed and ready to further boost the treasured Computer History Museum to new heights.

The Documentary

Now that I've perhaps whetted your appetite about watching Look Who's Driving, let's take a peek under-the-hood of this soon to be released documentary.

Spoiler alert: I'm going to be identifying various detailed aspects of the documentary, which I suppose might somewhat dampen the surprise when you watch it, but I assure you that a picture is worth a thousand words, thus my review doesn't undercut the visually powerful impact of your watching the actual film.

First, pretend that you sitting in the movie theatre there at the Computer History Museum, the lights have just dimmed, the crowd has gone quiet with anticipation, and the film softly begins to roll.

Screech!

Bam!

A perceptible gasp arose in the theater as the now-infamous Uber self-driving car incident that occurred last year, sadly taking the life of a pedestrian, glaringly and loudly fills your senses, including gritty tough-to-watch snippets of video recorded at the time.

That's the eye-popping opening scene of the film.

This incident is unabashedly front and center and a recurring talking point throughout the film.

Whereas many documentaries on driverless cars ease the viewer gingerly into the topic of self-driving cars, gradually leading up to what many consider the watershed-like moment of the Uber case, instead we are essentially face smacked at the start of the story being told here.

I was initially concerned that perhaps the opener would become a preoccupation with the "badness" of self-driving car efforts and overly permeate the entire narrative.

As the documentary unfolds, it becomes readily apparent that the opener was an instrumental foil to address both the ups and downs of driverless car efforts.

Rather than hiding the elephant in the room about driverless cars, it makes sense to tackle the Uber case straight ahead. Those that are only vaguely familiar with what happened or weren't even aware of the incident are appropriately teed up.

In essence, I favor getting on the table the "dirty laundry" right away, prodding viewers headfirst into a warranted mode of being alert and mindfully attentive. Coverage that begins in a lighter and rosy world of The Jetsons wonderment cannot sufficiently drive home the notion that this is real-world stuff with real-world consequences.

At the screening, I spoke with the writers and producers about the documentary, including Kiki Kapany (CEO of Kikim Media) and Edward Gray (Producer-Director-Writer at Kikim Media), and discussed their gruelingly tortuous choices in putting together the film.

It is no easy task to try and boil down the myriad of complex aspects of self-driving cars into a mere half-hour of viewing time.

Of course, for those that are accustomed to TikTok videos as their primary source of info about mankind, consisting of clips that last less than the time it takes to brush your teeth, a half-hour is an eternity (well, unless it involves kittens and puppies romping around).

Today's viewers aren't going to watch a documentary end-to-end unless there is a compelling and engaging arc and a pulsating pace to keep viewers actively immersed.

Labeling something as a "documentary" can be its death-knell for a generation raised on mindless YouTube videos and instant gratification text messaging.

Overall, I completely agree with this purposeful cinematic positioning of the prominent Uber incident as a key grabber at the start, which is directly followed by a richness of expert opinions and important contextual considerations to further round out what can be learned from the matter.

As the documentary proceeds, seamless editing rapidly shifts into looking at the sobering fact that there are already a massive number of deaths and injuries occurring due to conventional human-based driving.

We all want to reduce the body count, and driverless cars offer that promise.

For those aching to get to zero fatalities due to the advent of self-driving, I've exhorted repeatedly that zero fatalities are a zero chance.

The panel later in the evening echoed this same point, and if society is only willing to accept zero fatalities as an arbiter of success, we'll likely never see driverless cars emerge (see my explanation in this piece).

Don't get stuck on the number zero.

Focus instead on the word safety.

Safety is the crucial catchword in the self-driving acrimonious debate.

The documentary addresses the question of what safety means and how will the definition of safeness shape the path and outcome for arriving at driverless cars.

Tackling numerous existing controversies, acclaimed Elon Musk and Tesla get airtime that on the one hand depicts the immense fan praise of Tesla devotees, yet we also get to see the Tesla automobile accidents that have involved the use of Autopilot.

I was pleased too in seeing a discussion about the moniker "Autopilot," for which critics assert that the chosen name is a blatant branding ploy, flagrantly overstating what the Tesla software can do (though Musk asserts the name is rightfully on-par). The documentary vividly points out that drivers are often misled about the driving abilities of the tech, tending to watch videos or play board games when their full attention instead should be on the driving task.

This misimpression by drivers is not solely as a result of the name conflation.

As known by insiders and as expressed by the experts included in the film (most of whom are colleagues and it was nice to see them featured on the big screen), driver inattention is also due to drivers that routinely use semi-autonomous features and begin to falsely think those capabilities are advanced enough to let the car drive on its own.

Insidiously, if you use such a feature and it seems to work, again and again, you fall into the cognitive trap that it will prevail all of the time (a classic statistical foible).

Inch by inch, you become less attuned to the driving task. This is a nearly inevitable consequence that I have forewarned is going to make for a horrific result as automakers brazenly roll out Level 3 semi-autonomous cars.

Speaking of Tesla, I might have hoped to see coverage about Musk's repeated eschewing of LIDAR and how nearly everyone else disagrees with the anti-LIDAR posture, especially since the film includes a sizable chunk of time devoted to LIDAR capabilities, but presumably there is only so much that can be crammed into a half-hour (for my analysis about why the anti-LIDAR camp is treading on thin ground, read my post here).

The Panel

On the topic of treasured colleagues, the assembled panel of luminaries provided a spirited discussion after the film was previewed.

Consisting of longtime members of the relatively short history of self-driving cars (historically, many cite the DARPA series of self-driving car challenges as a crucial inflection point, starting in 2004), the esteemed panel offered insights about where we've been, how we got here, and what the future might be.

Moderated by Professor Talithia Williams of Harvey Mudd College, she offered a plethora of probing questions to the panelists.

With her charisma and seemingly effortless fireside chat style, the panelists were prodded into discussing now-classic kinds of questions (e.g., when can we expect to have true self-driving cars, how can we we trust the AI), and even extended beyond the usual confront zone by including thorny questions that lurk in the recesses of many minds (i.e., could someone command the AI to intentionally run over a person in front of the vehicle if they are threatening those inside the car).

As a panelist, Dmitri Dolgov, CTO and VP of Engineering at Waymo, articulated the motivations for achieving self-driving cars in response to a question about why numerous tech firms and automakers are pursuing these endeavors.

Besides the hoped-for life savings by doing away with the chances of drunk drivers and untoward human shortcomings of driving, he also talked about Waymo's persistent focus on Level 4 and Level 5 self-driving cars.

Early on, Google launched a number of next-gen swing-for-the-fence initiatives, including what has evolved into today's Waymo entity, and in their initial foray, the researchers and developers realized that trying to contend with the semi-autonomous arena and its human co-sharing drivers would become a mired muddle, potentially perturbing and inhibiting efforts to stride toward true driverless cars.

As such, Waymo is deeply focused on true self-driving cars, a kind of leapfrog strategy versus the stepwise approach being undertaken by many others to first achieve semi-autonomous Level 2 and Level 3 cars and then make progress toward Level 4 and Level 5.

Dmitri's expressed that one of his favored watchwords is tenacity, meaning that it takes a tenacious approach to keep making progress on the outreached goal of arriving at true self-driving cars.

Another panelist, Professor Chris Gerdes of Stanford University, added to the rationale for seeking self-driving cars by pointing out the likely possibility that mobility will increase significantly throughout society and be a transformational boon.

In locales that today could be considered as transit deserts, consisting of places lacking in viable options for transport, driverless cars could offer much-needed mobility-for-all relief.

This is reminiscent of the annual Princeton Summit on self-driving for the mobility marginalized that I've supported and often touted as a vital voice for infusing such considerations into today's driverless tech developments.

Professor Gerdes served as the first-ever Chief Innovation Officer for the U.S. Department of Transportation (DOT) and is co-founder of the truck platooning firm Peloton Technology. His combination of academic, commercial, and governmental experiences enabled a discussion about what role we might expect governments to play in self-driving car pursuits (an ongoing topic of complex deliberation).

Jesse Levinson, co-founder and CTO at Zoox (see my piece on his indubitably sensible mantra about remote driving not being a safety use case), offered the provocative point that safety can be a differentiator among competing self-driving car incarnations.

I appreciate Jesse's at-times provocateur comments since they often spark valuable discussions on the evolving nature of the self-driving car industry.

In this case, he was referring to the belief by some that all self-driving cars will need to be 100% safe, all of the time, and in any and all driving scenarios. If you believe that must be so, presumably there will be no differentiation between one vendor's self-driving car and another.

You might say they would all be fungible commodities with respect to safety.

I don't buy into that version of the future.

The real-world has such a diversity of driving circumstances that it would seem more likely that one vendor's driverless car might well be "safer" than another in certain use cases.

The idea that all self-driving cars will all work in essentially the same way and be at the same safety levels is not especially realistic.

That being said, the usual retort is that this implies a driverless car can somehow throw caution to the wind and be essentially unsafe whenever it pleases.

Not so.

There will undoubtedly be a societal "acceptable" threshold at which safeness must occur, and then entertain variability in heightened magnitudes of safeness above that threshold.

Of course, this won't be an easy messaging element.

Safety will be a razor's edge topic with the public.

You might recall that for many years the automotive industry would not utter the word "safety" in any of their marketing, worrying that doing so would alarm the public and instead the focus was on comfort, style, and performance of cars.

Eventually, and only gradually, safety emerged as a fair game topic, and today oftentimes is the core marketing claim to fame of some automobiles and automakers.

For self-driving cars, the odds are that we're going to have to start with safety, and only after a long period of assimilation and familiarization will we get onto other topics about driverless car capabilities and possibilities.

Jesse's watchword for the night was "why," meaning that we would all be wise to keep asking why in whatever we do since it is common to allow unstated assumptions to rule our behavior and for which we might be doing better if we questioned what we were doing.

Jack Weast, Senior Principal Engineer at Intel and Vice President of Automated Vehicle standards at Mobileye, pointed out that the way to gain trust about self-driving tech is to make sure that the industry remains open and transparent.

This is indeed an important banner that needs to be carried by all entrants and participants in the race toward driverless cars.

Society is unlikely to embrace self-driving cars, and might, in fact, stifle such efforts, if the driverless car companies seem to be trying to pull the wool over the eyes of those outside the industry.

Jack also emphasized the societal transformations that we can predict might accompany the adoption of self-driving cars. As a heartfelt example of aiding those that might at times be mobility disadvantaged, he told a story about his father having had knee surgery, becoming temporarily unable to drive a car and essentially stranded into immobility.

Imagine a day when a self-driving car could arrive and be used by someone that is unable to drive.

Rather than being trapped into immobility, the use of driverless cars could open a mobility capacity that would dramatically change people's lives and allow society as a whole to be free of today's friction-heavy limits on mobility.

Conclusion

Mark your calendar for the evening of October 23, 2019, to watch the Look Who's Driving documentary (well, either watch it when it premieres, being the first on your block to do so, or at least set-aside time soon thereafter to stream it when you can).

I pledge that you will find it to be informative, entertaining, frightening, uplifting, etc., and the content will satiate you with superb food-for-thought about self-driving cars.

Won't that be much more rewarding than watching a YouTube personality eating as many pancakes as they can stuff into their gut in a half-hour?

Given that self-driving cars will impact all our lives, best to choose the driverless car video over the pancake gorging one.

That's IMHO.

CHAPTER 13

BIRTHRATE CHANGES

AND

AI SELF-DRIVING CARS

CHAPTER 13
BIRTHRATE CHANGES
AND
AI SELF-DRIVING CARS

The latest stats from the Center for Disease Control (CDC) indicate that the birthrate in the United States has continued to decline, inching down to the lowest in 32 years, and this closely watched fertility indicator is predicted to continue going further down.

Numerically, the rate has become 1.72, based on data that shows there are now 59 births per 1,000 women in the U.S., statistically bounded by the age groups from 15 to 44 years old (considered the childbearing years, per how the CDC defines these matters).

The birthrate in America has been on an overall downward slope since the Great Recession started in 2008.

Why care that the birthrate is so low and seemingly going to go even lower?

One concern voiced by many demographic experts is that we need to achieve a birthrate of at least 2.1 to ensure the ongoing renewal of our population.

Yes, you read that correctly, namely that if we want to keep the United States population in good stead, we are supposed to be aiming at a birthrate of 2.1, otherwise, the aggregate number of deaths exceeds the number of births. When the deaths are exceeding births, the total population size decreases.

As the population size decreases, we have fewer and fewer people to shoulder the burdens of our society. Analysts decry that the United States is becoming an "aging society" of those over the age of 65 exceeding the number of those under the age of 15 (on a respective proportional basis).

So, we're now at a record low of 1.72 birthrate factor and somehow are supposed to find our way up to a 2.1, though all signs point in the other direction.

A crass remark by some would be that we need to set aside more effort toward procreating, which perhaps might be an opening line if you are half-drunk in a seedy bar.

Well, it is conceivable that something is going to happen in our society that will cause an uptick in the birthrate, though at first thought it might seem counter intuitive as a kind of savior for this crucial non-extinction qualm.

Here's the somewhat surprising solution: The advent of true self-driving cars might end-up boosting the birthrate in America.

Say what?

Let's unpack the matter.

The Levels Of Self-Driving Cars

It is important to clarify what I mean when referring to true self-driving cars.

True self-driving cars are ones that the AI drives the car entirely on its own and there isn't any human assistance during the driving task.

These driverless cars are considered a Level 4 and Level 5, while a car that requires a human driver to co-share the driving effort is usually considered at a Level 2 or Level 3. The cars that co-share the driving task are described as being semi-autonomous, and typically contain a variety of automated add-ons that are referred to as ADAS (Advanced Driver-Assistance Systems).

There is not yet a true self-driving car at Level 5, which we don't yet even know if this will be possible to achieve, and nor how long it will take to get there.

Meanwhile, the Level 4 efforts are gradually trying to get some traction by undergoing very narrow and selective public roadway trials, though there is controversy over whether this testing should be allowed per se (we are all life-or-death guinea pigs in an experiment taking place on our highways and byways, some point out).

Since the semi-autonomous cars require a human driver, such cars aren't particularly significant to this birthrate matter. There is essentially no difference between using a Level 2 or Level 3 versus a conventional car when it comes to driving and therefore doesn't merit discussion on this topic.

It is notable to point out that in spite of those dolts that keep posting videos of themselves falling asleep at the wheel of a Level 2 or Level 3 car, do not be misled into believing that you can take away your attention from the driving task while driving a semi-autonomous car.

You are the responsible party for the driving actions of the car, regardless of how much automation might be tossed into a Level 2 or Level 3.

Focus On True Self-Driving Cars

Let's go ahead and focus on the Level 4 and Level 5 autonomous cars.

There isn't a human driver needed in a true self-driving car, which though may be obvious, it is worthwhile to ponder the ramifications of no longer having human drivers in cars.

A human driver is normally an adult.

Besides driving the car, the adult driver also acts as a kind of supervisor overseeing any activity inside the car.

No monkey business is usually the rule that most adult drivers would offer to any younger occupants inside the vehicle.

Plus, the adult driver aids in determining where the car is going to go.

I'm leading you toward a point of importance that pertains to the birthrate matter.

With true self-driving cars, young people will be able to ride around without any direct adult supervision in the vehicle. Furthermore, those young people can presumably tell the AI to go here or there, wherever they might wish to have the AI system drive them.

Some believe that we might open a pandora's box by providing a "safe place" for young people to do certain kinds of deeds if you get my drift.

Two youths that eyed each other at school are aiming to have a private rendezvous. In today's world, they would need to likely get their respective parents to give them a lift, and presumably, need to tell their parents where they will be going.

Such spying eyes by the parents make any private activity less likely to readily occur.

In the future, one of the two youths can access a mobile app to request a self-driving car ride, jump into the empty driverless car once it arrives, take it to pick-up the other youth, and they now have a place to get to know each other (wink-wink).

If the two need some extended private time, they could tell the AI to drive around town a couple of times, not aiming to go anywhere in particular. Essentially, they are in a roving capsule that innocuously makes its way across town.

Many are expecting that self-driving cars won't have regular windows, and will instead have LED displays, allowing you to watch a movie or see streaming videos while inside the driverless car. As such, the inside activity of the self-driving car will be blocked from view by those outside of the vehicle.

This certainly seems ready-made for hanky panky.

Suppose though that the number of miles being driven is tracked and going to be charged to the parent's credit card. Those darned parents are eventually going to ask untoward questions about why the self-driving car was randomly roaming around the city.

If that's a potential hiccup in the youthful interest of being together, they could tell the AI system to take them to a remote locale, park there, and afford some personal time for the occupants, or maybe drop them off and come back later to pick them up.

With amorous teens, where there's a will, there's a way.

I don't want to make it seem as though the youth of America will be the only ones leveraging the self-driving car capabilities for such purposes.

Imagine that you use an online dating service to find a potential match.

Nowadays, after doing some amount of online courtship, you likely agree to meet in-person.

In Los Angeles, many people won't even start to date someone that lives more than about fifteen to twenty miles away, because the drive time is horrendous. They know that despite a potential match made in heaven, it won't work if they each have to endure bumper-to-bumper traffic for an hour each way to see each other.

One of the most touted advantages of self-driving cars is that they will open wide a new era of mobility.

Some are referring to the emergence of driverless cars as shifting our economy into one based on friction-free mobility. The catchword or emerging phrase is mobility-for-all.

Thus, after you find an online connection that you feel is suited for you, the act of getting together will be a lot easier than it is today.

You merely request a lift from a self-driving car and have it drive you to your potential sweetheart. You don't need to do the driving. You don't need to cope with the crushing stress of driving in nightmarish traffic. Instead, sit back and relax, contemplating how much joy you'll have to get to your hoped-for true love.

Notice that this use case does not involve any hanky panky inside the driverless car.

As such, the self-driving car is not serving as a den of debauchery, and instead simply aiding in upping the chances of people being able to get to see each other in-person.

In somewhat crude terms, what does it take to procreate?

In theory, you need to have access and opportunity.

Self-driving cars will provide ready-made access and enable ready-made opportunities.

The barrier to dating will be eased. People of ardent interest can go see each other, whenever they wish, using non-stop 24x7 available self-driving cars. Face to face time will dramatically increase.

This all could make the world a better place, encouraging more human-to-human interaction that goes beyond using Facetime and text messaging.

Oops, more in-person human-to-human interaction can have another result, specifically the ability to let passions rein.

Conclusion

The advent of true self-driving cars has several compelling elements that suggest the birthrate could very well reverse in decline and start to head-up.

You might be relieved to know that his potential new trend in the birthrate could be stymied despite the emergence of driverless cars.

First, it is anticipated that true self-driving cars are going to have cameras facing inward, doing so to curtail riders that might want to mark graffiti in the driverless car or otherwise destroy the interior and be caught on film doing so.

Those cameras will serve other helpful purposes too, such as parents being able to send their kids to school in a self-driving car, absent any adult in the car, and watch their kids during their journey, making sure they safely reach school.

In that case, the youths that want to play some private games inside a self-driving car are going to be on candid camera. Even if there is a feature allowing occupants to turn off the cameras, I'm sure that doting parents are going to insist that the cameras remain turned on the entire time that those youths are being carted around.

Overall, it certainly would seem vital to society that self-driving cars not become a place for underage untoward acts, since we all likely would be disturbed to have underage births becoming a more commonplace matter.

Strikeout then the potential for youthful indiscretions, but you can still keep into the mix the notion that mobility will be expanded. The odds are that the wider mobility is going to dominate the access and opportunity factors anyway.

One of the assumed reasons that there has been an ongoing decline in the U.S. birthrate is due to people being more attuned to using protective methods. If the culture keeps that attention going, presumably added access and opportunity won't lead to an increase in the birthrate.

It could be that driverless cars might include protecting methods in the vehicle for the convenience of passengers' use, for those that might get an urge and seek to leverage the driverless car for private purposes.

Some say that the economy is one of the largest factors in determining birthrates.

When the economy tanks, people don't want to add the burden and costs of having children.

It's hard to say whether self-driving cars in themselves will spark the economy, which some economists believe will be the case. If so, it would presumably tend to grease the skids on upping the birthrate. The economy though has so many moving parts that it is problematic to assert that driverless cars will be the sole or primary factor for an economic boom, but it could be a handy spark.

Another consideration would be the parental drain when having children and having to contend with work and raising a child.

Perhaps driverless cars will make it easier to take your children to work with you since you won't be driving the car and can completely attend to your child during the commute. Also, for those that might have a nanny or similar come to their homes for childcare, the use of driverless cars could make it a lot easier to get someone to come to your domicile to watch over your kids.

All in all, I'd put my money on the bet that true self-driving cars will spur the birthrate to turnaround and head upward. I don't see the upward movement as a runaway train and anticipate that once we all get used to driverless cars, life will settle in and we'll stabilize in many ways that at first got jumbled or rejiggered.

Does this mean that we all should be cheering for self-driving cars to get here soonest, allowing us to achieve the vaunted 2.1 birthrate?

I'll let you decide that.

APPENDIX

APPENDIX A
TEACHING WITH THIS MATERIAL

The material in this book can be readily used either as a supplemental to other content for a class, or it can also be used as a core set of textbook material for a specialized class. Classes where this material is most likely used include any classes at the college or university level that want to augment the class by offering thought provoking and educational essays about AI and self-driving cars.

In particular, here are some aspects for class use:

o   Computer Science. Studying AI, autonomous vehicles, etc.

o   Business. Exploring technology and it adoption for business.

o   Sociology. Sociological views on the adoption and advancement of technology.

Specialized classes at the undergraduate and graduate level can also make use of this material.

For each chapter, consider whether you think the chapter provides material relevant to your course topic. There is plenty of opportunity to get the students thinking about the topic and force them to decide whether they agree or disagree with the points offered and positions taken. I would also encourage you to have the students do additional research beyond the chapter material presented (I provide next some suggested assignments they can do).

RESEARCH ASSIGNMENTS ON THESE TOPICS

Your students can find background material on these topics, doing so in various business and technical publications. I list below the top ranked AI related journals. For business publications, I would suggest the usual culprits such as the Harvard Business Review, Forbes, Fortune, WSJ, and the like.

Here are some suggestions of homework or projects that you could assign to students:

a) Assignment for foundational AI research topic: Research and prepare a paper and a presentation on a specific aspect of Deep AI, Machine Learning, ANN, etc. The paper should cite at least 3 reputable sources. Compare and contrast to what has been stated in this book.

b) Assignment for the Self-Driving Car topic: Research and prepare a paper and Self-Driving Cars. Cite at least 3 reputable sources and analyze the characterizations. Compare and contrast to what has been stated in this book.

c) Assignment for a Business topic: Research and prepare a paper and a presentation on businesses and advanced technology. What is hot, and what is not? Cite at least 3 reputable sources. Compare and contrast to the depictions in this book.

d) Assignment to do a Startup: Have the students prepare a paper about how they might startup a business in this realm. They must submit a sound Business Plan for the startup. They could also be asked to present their Business Plan and so should also have a presentation deck to coincide with it.

You can certainly adjust the aforementioned assignments to fit to your particular needs and the class structure. You'll notice that I ask for 3 reputable cited sources for the paper writing based assignments. I usually steer students toward "reputable" publications, since otherwise they will cite some oddball source that has no credentials other than that they happened to write something and post it onto the Internet. You can define "reputable" in whatever way you prefer, for example some faculty think Wikipedia is not reputable while others believe it is reputable and allow students to cite it.

The reason that I usually ask for at least 3 citations is that if the student only does one or two citations they usually settle on whatever they happened to find the fastest. By requiring three citations, it usually seems to force them to look around, explore, and end-up probably finding five or more, and then whittling it down to 3 that they will actually use.

I have not specified the length of their papers, and leave that to you to tell the students what you prefer. For each of those assignments, you could end-up with a short one to two pager, or you could do a dissertation length paper. Base the length on whatever best fits for your class, and the credit amount of the assignment within the context of the other grading metrics you'll be using for the class.

I mention in the assignments that they are to do a paper and prepare a presentation. I usually try to get students to present their work. This is a good practice for what they will do in the business world. Most of the time, they will be required to prepare an analysis and present it. If you don't have the class time or inclination to have the students present, then you can of course cut out the aspect of them putting together a presentation.

If you want to point students toward highly ranked journals in AI, here's a list of the top journals as reported by *various citation counts sources* (this list changes year to year):

- o   Communications of the ACM
- o   Artificial Intelligence
- o   Cognitive Science
- o   IEEE Transactions on Pattern Analysis and Machine Intelligence
- o   Foundations and Trends in Machine Learning
- o   Journal of Memory and Language
- o   Cognitive Psychology
- o   Neural Networks
- o   IEEE Transactions on Neural Networks and Learning Systems
- o   IEEE Intelligent Systems
- o   Knowledge-based Systems

GUIDE TO USING THE CHAPTERS

For each of the chapters, I provide next some various ways to use the chapter material. You can assign the tasks as individual homework assignments, or the tasks can be used with team projects for the class. You can easily layout a series of assignments, such as indicating that the students are to do item "a" below for say Chapter 1, then "b" for the next chapter of the book, and so on.

a) What is the main point of the chapter and describe in your own words the significance of the topic,

b) Identify at least two aspects in the chapter that you agree with, and support your concurrence by providing at least one other outside researched item as support; make sure to explain your basis for disagreeing with the aspects,

c) Identify at least two aspects in the chapter that you disagree with, and support your disagreement by providing at least one other outside researched item as support; make sure to explain your basis for disagreeing with the aspects,

d) Find an aspect that was not covered in the chapter, doing so by conducting outside research, and then explain how that aspect ties into the chapter and what significance it brings to the topic,

e) Interview a specialist in industry about the topic of the chapter, collect from them their thoughts and opinions, and readdress the chapter by citing your source and how they compared and contrasted to the material,

f) Interview a relevant academic professor or researcher in a college or university about the topic of the chapter, collect from them their thoughts and opinions, and readdress the chapter by citing your source and how they compared and contrasted to the material,

g) Try to update a chapter by finding out the latest on the topic, and ascertain whether the issue or topic has now been solved or whether it is still being addressed, explain what you come up with.

The above are all ways in which you can get the students of your class involved in considering the material of a given chapter. You could mix things up by having one of those above assignments per each week, covering the chapters over the course of the semester or quarter.

As a reminder, here are the chapters of the book and you can select whichever chapters you find most valued for your particular class:

Chapter Title

1   Eliot Framework for AI Self-Driving Cars

2   Solving Loneliness and AI Self-Driving Cars

3   Headless Issues and AI Self-Driving Cars

4   Roaming Empty and AI Self-Driving Cars

5   Millennials Exodus and AI Self-Driving Cars

6   Recession Worries and AI Self-Driving Cars

7   Remote Operation Issues and AI Self-Driving Cars

8   Boomerang Kids and AI Self-Driving Cars

9   Waymo Coming To L.A. and AI Self-Driving Cars

10   Getting To Scale and AI Self-Driving Cars

11   Looking Alike and AI Self-Driving Cars

12   NOVA Documentary On AI Self-Driving Cars

13   Birthrate Changes and AI Self-Driving Cars

Companion Book By This Author

Advances in AI and Autonomous Vehicles: Cybernetic Self-Driving Cars

Practical Advances in Artificial Intelligence (AI) and Machine Learning
by
Dr. Lance B. Eliot, MBA, PhD

This title is available via Amazon and other book sellers

Companion Book By This Author

Self-Driving Cars:
"The Mother of All AI Projects"

by Dr. Lance B. Eliot, MBA, PhD

Chapter Title

This title is available via Amazon and other book sellers

Companion Book By This Author

Innovation and Thought Leadership
on Self-Driving Driverless Cars

by Dr. Lance B. Eliot, MBA, PhD

This title is available via Amazon and other book sellers

<u>Companion Book By This Author</u>

New Advances in AI Autonomous Driverless Cars Self-Driving Cars

by Dr. Lance B. Eliot, MBA, PhD

<u>Chapter Title</u>

This title is available via Amazon and other book sellers

Companion Book By This Author

Introduction to
Driverless Self-Driving Cars

by Dr. Lance B. Eliot, MBA, PhD

Chapter Title

This title is available via Amazon and other book sellers

Companion Book By This Author
Autonomous Vehicle Driverless Self-Driving Cars and Artificial Intelligence
by Dr. Lance B. Eliot, MBA, PhD

This title is available via Amazon and other book sellers

Companion Book By This Author

Transformative Artificial Intelligence Driverless Self-Driving Cars

by Dr. Lance B. Eliot, MBA, PhD

Chapter Title

This title is available via Amazon and other book sellers

Companion Book By This Author

Disruptive Artificial Intelligence
and Driverless Self-Driving Cars

by Dr. Lance B. Eliot, MBA, PhD

This title is available via Amazon and other book sellers

Companion Book By This Author

State-of-the-Art
AI Driverless Self-Driving Cars

by Dr. Lance B. Eliot, MBA, PhD

Chapter Title

This title is available via Amazon and other book sellers

Companion Book By This Author

Top Trends in
AI Self-Driving Cars

by Dr. Lance B. Eliot, MBA, PhD

Chapter Title

1　Eliot Framework for AI Self-Driving Cars

2　Responsibility and Self-Driving Cars

3　Changing Lanes and Self-Driving Cars

4　Procrastination and Self-Driving Cars

5　NTSB Report and Tesla Car Crash

6　Start Over AI and Self-Driving Cars

7　Freezing Robot Problem and Self-Driving Cars

8　Canarying and Self-Driving Cars

9　Nighttime Driving and Self-Driving Cars

10　Zombie-Cars Taxes and Self-Driving Cars

11　Traffic Lights and Self-Driving Cars

12　Reverse Engineering and Self-Driving Cars

13　Singularity AI and Self-Driving Cars

This title is available via Amazon and other book sellers

Companion Book By This Author

AI Innovations
and Self-Driving Cars

by Dr. Lance B. Eliot, MBA, PhD

This title is available via Amazon and other book sellers

This title is available via Amazon and other book sellers

Companion Book By This Author

Sociotechnical Insights and AI Driverless Cars

by Dr. Lance B. Eliot, MBA, PhD

Chapter Title

This title is available via Amazon and other book sellers

<u>Companion Book By This Author</u>

Pioneering Advances for AI Driverless Cars

by Dr. Lance B. Eliot, MBA, PhD

<u>Chapter Title</u>

This title is available via Amazon and other book sellers

Companion Book By This Author

Leading Edge Trends for AI Driverless Cars

by Dr. Lance B. Eliot, MBA, PhD

This title is available via Amazon and other book sellers

Companion Book By This Author

The Cutting Edge of
AI Autonomous Cars

by Dr. Lance B. Eliot, MBA, PhD

This title is available via Amazon and other book sellers

Companion Book By This Author

The Next Wave of
AI Self-Driving Cars

by Dr. Lance B. Eliot, MBA, PhD

Chapter Title

This title is available via Amazon and other book sellers

Companion Book By This Author

Revolutionary Innovations of AI Self-Driving Cars

by Dr. Lance B. Eliot, MBA, PhD

Chapter Title

This title is available via Amazon and other book sellers

Companion Book By This Author

AI Self-Driving Cars
Breakthroughs

by Dr. Lance B. Eliot, MBA, PhD

Chapter Title

This title is available via Amazon and other book sellers

Companion Book By This Author

Trailblazing Trends for AI Self-Driving Cars

by Dr. Lance B. Eliot, MBA, PhD

This title is available via Amazon and other book sellers

<u>Companion Book By This Author</u>

Ingenious Strides for
AI Driverless Cars

by Dr. Lance B. Eliot, MBA, PhD

<u>Chapter Title</u>

This title is available via Amazon and other book sellers

Companion Book By This Author

AI Self-Driving Cars
Inventiveness

by Dr. Lance B. Eliot, MBA, PhD

This title is available via Amazon and other book sellers

Companion Book By This Author

Visionary Secrets of
AI Driverless Cars

by Dr. Lance B. Eliot, MBA, PhD

Chapter Title

This title is available via Amazon and other book sellers

Companion Book By This Author

Spearheading AI Self-Driving Cars

by Dr. Lance B. Eliot, MBA, PhD

This title is available via Amazon and other book sellers

Companion Book By This Author

Spurring
AI Self-Driving Cars
by Dr. Lance B. Eliot, MBA, PhD

Chapter Title

This title is available via Amazon and other book sellers

Companion Book By This Author

Avant-Garde
AI Driverless Cars

by Dr. Lance B. Eliot, MBA, PhD

This title is available via Amazon and other book sellers

Companion Book By This Author

AI Self-Driving Cars
Evolvement

by Dr. Lance B. Eliot, MBA, PhD

This title is available via Amazon and other book sellers

Companion Book By This Author

AI Driverless Cars Chrysalis
by Dr. Lance B. Eliot, MBA, PhD

<u>Chapter Title</u>

1 Eliot Framework for AI Self-Driving Cars

2 Object Poses and AI Self-Driving Cars

3 Human In-The-Loop and AI Self-Driving Cars

4 Genius Shortage and AI Self-Driving Cars

5 Salvage Yards and AI Self-Driving Cars

6 Precision Scheduling and AI Self-Driving Car

7 Human Driving Extinction and AI Self-Driving Cars

This title is available via Amazon and other book sellers

<u>Companion Book By This Author</u>

Boosting
AI Autonomous Cars
by Dr. Lance B. Eliot, MBA, PhD

<u>Chapter Title</u>

This title is available via Amazon and other book sellers

Companion Book By This Author

AI Self-Driving Cars Trendsetting

by Dr. Lance B. Eliot, MBA, PhD

This title is available via Amazon and other book sellers

Companion Book By This Author

AI Autonomous Cars Forefront

by Dr. Lance B. Eliot, MBA, PhD

Chapter Title

This title is available via Amazon and other book sellers

<u>Companion Book By This Author</u>

AI Autonomous Cars Emergence

by Dr. Lance B. Eliot, MBA, PhD

<u>Chapter Title</u>

This title is available via Amazon and other book sellers

Companion Book By This Author

AI Autonomous Cars Progress

by Dr. Lance B. Eliot, MBA, PhD

This title is available via Amazon and other book sellers

<u>Companion Book By This Author</u>

AI Self-Driving Cars
Prognosis

by Dr. Lance B. Eliot, MBA, PhD

<u>Chapter Title</u>

This title is available via Amazon and other book sellers

Companion Book By This Author

AI Autonomous Cars Momentum

by Dr. Lance B. Eliot, MBA, PhD

This title is available via Amazon and other book sellers

ABOUT THE AUTHOR

Dr. Lance B. Eliot, MBA, PhD is the CEO of Techbruim, Inc. and Executive Director of the Cybernetic AI Self-Driving Car Institute and has over twenty years of industry experience including serving as a corporate officer in a billion dollar firm and was a partner in a major executive services firm. He is also a serial entrepreneur having founded, ran, and sold several high-tech related businesses. He previously hosted the popular radio show *Technotrends* that was also available on American Airlines flights via their in-flight audio program. Author or co-author of a dozen books and over 400 articles, he has made appearances on CNN, and has been a frequent speaker at industry conferences.

A former professor at the University of Southern California (USC), he founded and led an innovative research lab on Artificial Intelligence in Business. Known as the "AI Insider" his writings on AI advances and trends has been widely read and cited. He also previously served on the faculty of the University of California Los Angeles (UCLA), and was a visiting professor at other major universities. He was elected to the International Board of the Society for Information Management (SIM), a prestigious association of over 3,000 high-tech executives worldwide.

He has performed extensive community service, including serving as Senior Science Adviser to the Vice Chair of the Congressional Committee on Science & Technology. He has served on the Board of the OC Science & Engineering Fair (OCSEF), where he is also has been a Grand Sweepstakes judge, and likewise served as a judge for the Intel International SEF (ISEF). He served as the Vice Chair of the Association for Computing Machinery (ACM) Chapter, a prestigious association of computer scientists. Dr. Eliot has been a shark tank judge for the USC Mark Stevens Center for Innovation on start-up pitch competitions, and served as a mentor for several incubators and accelerators in Silicon Valley and Silicon Beach. He served on several Boards and Committees at USC, including having served on the Marshall Alumni Association (MAA) Board in Southern California.

Dr. Eliot holds a PhD from USC, MBA, and Bachelor's in Computer Science, and earned the CDP, CCP, CSP, CDE, and CISA certifications. Born and raised in Southern California, and having traveled and lived internationally, he enjoys scuba diving, surfing, and sailing.

ADDENDUM

AI Self-Driving Cars Momentum

Practical Advances in Artificial Intelligence (AI) and Machine Learning

By
Dr. Lance B. Eliot, MBA, PhD

———

For supplemental materials of this book, visit:
www.ai-selfdriving-cars.guru

For special orders of this book, contact:
LBE Press Publishing
Email: LBE.Press.Publishing@gmail.com

www.ingramcontent.com/pod-product-compliance
Lightning Source LLC
Chambersburg PA
CBHW051047050326
40690CB00006B/633